CHILDREN
Just Like Me

This book belongs to

Stick a photo of yourself here!

My name is

_____

Penguin Random House

Project art editor Fiona Macdonald
Project editor Sam Priddy
Photoshoot coordinators Katy Lennon
and Louise Tucker
US editor Margaret Parrish
Additional editing Jolyon Goddard, Katy Lennon,
Gill Pitts, and Kathleen Teece
Additional design Joanne Clark,
Rhea Gaughan, Emma Hobson, Stuart Jackman,
Faith Nelson, and Ala Uddin
Senior DTP designer Jagtar Singh
Managing editor Laura Gilbert
Managing art editor Diane Peyton Jones
Picture researcher Rob Nunn
Pre-production producer Nadine King
Producer Srijana Gurung
Art director Martin Wilson
Publisher Sarah Larter
Publishing director Sophie Mitchell

Written by Catherine Saunders, Sam Priddy,
and Katy Lennon
Consultant Robert Dinwiddie

First American Edition, 2016
Published in the United States by DK Publishing
1745 Broadway, 20th Floor, New York, NY 10019

DK books are available at special discounts when purchased in bulk
for sales promotions, premiums, fund-raising, or educational use.
For details, contact: DK Publishing Special Markets,
1745 Broadway, 20th Floor, New York, NY 10019
SpecialSales@dk.com

Printed in UAE

For the curious
www.dk.com

MIX
Paper from
responsible sources
FSC™ C018179

This book was made with Forest Stewardship
Council ™ certified paper—one small step
in DK's commitment to a sustainable future.
For more information go to www.dk.com/
our-green-pledge

Contents

4 Foreword

6 North America

8 Lauryn from Canada

9 Lily from the US

10 Andrea from the US

11 Joaquin from the US

12 Cymian from the US

14 Alonso from Mexico

16 South America

18 Rafael from Brazil

20 Trini from Argentina

22 Miguel from Colombia

24 Europe

26 Alec from England

27 Jack from Ireland

28 Mattus from Finland

29 Martyna from Poland

30 Solal from France

31 Morgan from France

32 Maria from Greece

33 Lucas from Spain

34 Clara from Germany

36 Stella from Sweden

37 Yaroslav from Russia

Meet the photographers

James
James took photos in Canada,
the US, Mexico, Brazil,
Argentina, Colombia, England,
France, Pakistan, Kazakhstan,
Australia, and New Zealand.

Mulugeta
Mulugeta took photos in Ethiopia.

Karin
Karin took photos in Botswana.

Idris
Idris took photos in China,
Mongolia, Japan, South Korea,
India, Israel, and Bahrain.

38 Africa

40 Bassma from Morocco

41 Yohanna from Ethiopia

42 Shigo from Tanzania

44 Joshua from Botswana

46 Jedidiah from Ghana

47 Hafsa from South Africa

48 Amu from South Africa

50 Asia

52 Shaowei from China

54 Robert from Mongolia

56 Sotaro from Japan

58 Yeh-Lin from South Korea

60 Mehak from India

61 Vishnu from India

62 Murk from Pakistan

64 Bolat from Kazakhstan

66 Erel from Israel

67 Khalifa from Bahrain

68 Southeast Asia and Australasia

70 Knight from Thailand

71 Ivan from Malaysia

72 Tai from Vietnam

74 Andre from Australia

75 Clara and Lucy from Australia

76 Jamie from New Zealand

78 Glossary

80 Index and Acknowledgments

Alan
Alan took photos in Morocco.

Andy
Andy took photos in England, Ireland, Finland, Poland, France, Greece, Germany, Sweden, Russia, Tanzania, Ghana, and South Africa.

Vinh
Vinh took photos in Thailand, Malaysia, and Vietnam.

Mike
Mike took photos in Spain.

Foreword

Welcome to this brand-new edition of *Children Just Like Me*—a celebration of children and childhood around the world. Since the first edition of *Children Just Like Me* was published in 1995 the world has changed a lot, and the children from the original book are now in their late twenties and early thirties. It felt like the right time to make a new edition of *Children Just Like Me*, which follows the children of today.

The children who are featured in this book come from a variety of countries and a range of different backgrounds. In many cases they appear to lead very different lives, whether it's dressing in different clothes or eating different kinds of foods. But they also play the same games, worry about the same things, and find the same things funny. The biggest realization we had making this book was that wherever they are in the world and whatever year it is, every child is unique and capable of great things. This book aims to celebrate them.

Sophie Mitchell.

Sophie Mitchell
DK Children's Publishing Director

Published in 1995

Published in 2016

Making a difference

Talking to children featured in this book we realized that many of them have similar concerns. What can you do to help? One way to help is by volunteering with or supporting a local charity. Buying this book helps kids, too. For each copy of *Children Just Like Me* sold, DK will donate a new, age-appropriate book to a child in need.

> "People should be nicer to animals and not treat them badly."

Education

Several of the children expressed concern that not all kids have access to an education. Through education, children can learn the skills needed to help their communities and make valuable contributions to society.

> "I would like all children to be able to go to school."

Mehak from India

Animal welfare

Many of the children we met worry about cruelty to animals. We were frequently told by children how saddened they are by the way animals are sometimes mistreated by people—from pets that are abused to turtles that can't survive in polluted oceans.

Lily from the US

The environment

Taking care of the environment is a much greater concern for children today than it was when the first edition of *Children Just Like Me* was published. Progress is slow, so it is crucial that children are encouraged to keep up the fight for a greener world.

> "I want to find a treatment for cancer."

Bolat from Kazakhstan

> "I would like to help all the people in poverty who can't afford basic needs."

> "I wish for a world with less deforestation."

Rafael from Brazil

Health care

When we asked the children in this book what jobs they want to do when they grow up, the same two answers kept coming up: doctors and nurses. Given the opportunity, children can promote healthy lifestyles in their communities and help prevent illness and disease.

Amu from South Africa

Poverty

Perhaps the biggest concern for the kids in this book is the plight of children less fortunate than them. It is crucial that children in impoverished communities are able to learn the skills to help them and their families impove their situation.

North America

North America stretches from the icy plains of Canada to the jungles and deserts of Central America and the islands of the Caribbean. In between is the United States, home to tribes that have lived there for thousands of years, as well as the descendants of settlers from Europe, Africa, and Asia.

Pancakes

Pancakes are a popular breakfast dish in the US and Canada. They are often served with maple syrup, sweet toppings, and fruit.

Mayan ruins

Deep within the rain forests of Mexico and Guatemala are amazing pyramids built by the Mayan people more than 1,000 years ago.

Grand Canyon

Cutting through the state of Arizona is the Grand Canyon, a giant gorge more than 5,906 ft (1,800 m) deep.

Grizzly bear

The forests of the US and Canada are home to grizzly bears—giant furry mammals that enjoy feasting on salmon.

Playing baseball

Baseball is a national pastime in North America. The goal of the game is to hit a ball with a bat and make it around the diamond to score runs, or points, for your team.

Canada
Find Lauryn on page 8

Alaska, USA

Ohio, USA
Find Lily on page 9

New Jersey, USA
Find Joaquin on page 11

Greenland
(Denmark)

Alaska

Canada

Montana, USA
Find Cymian on pages 12–13

Montana

USA

Ohio ○— New Jersey

California

Texas

○— South
Carolina

South Carolina, USA
Find Andrea on page 10

Haiti
Dominican
Republic

Cuba

Mexico

Belize

Jamaica

Guatemala
El Salvador
Nicaragua
Costa Rica

Panama

Texas, USA

California, USA

Mexico

Mexico
Find Alonso on pages 14–15

Guatemala

Nicaragua

Jamaica

Lauryn

Lauryn is eight years old and lives in Quebec, a French-speaking region of Canada. She speaks both English and French, and at school half her classes are in French and the other half are in English. Lauryn loves animals and has nine pets! They are a cat, a snake, three guinea pigs, a hamster, and three ferrets.

Lauryn and her dad

Lauryn sees her dad, Sandy, every weekend. They speak to each other in English. Sandy is an air traffic controller. He helps aircraft pilots take off and land safely.

Sandy
father

Lauryn

This ferret's name is Atchoum, which is French for "sneezy."

Weekday home

During the week, Lauryn lives with her mom, Armelle, and her stepfather, Éric. His children, Kiana and Gaël, also live with them for some of the time.

Lauryn's house

Éric
stepfather

Armelle
mother

Kiana
stepsister

Lauryn

Gaël
stepbrother

Poutine

Chicken wings

Canadian specialty

Poutine is a popular dish in Quebec. It's made of fries with cheese curds and light gravy, and it tastes great with grilled chicken wings.

Signature

Lauryn

How I say hello

Bonjour
Pronounced "bon-JHOOR"

Where I live

Lauryn lives on the outskirts of Montreal, which is the largest city in Quebec.

Montreal

Montreal is the second-biggest city in Canada. More than 4 million people live in the city and its suburbs.

"If I could change anything in the world, I would turn all the sidewalks into trampolines!"

Lily and her younger brother, Ridge, are wearing their Halloween costumes.

Lily

Seven-year-old Lily lives on a farm in Ohio. She enjoys dressing up, especially for Halloween, but she wears old clothes when helping on the farm. Lily loves animals, especially her pet cat, Kitty Soft Paws, and her hobbies include dancing and acrobatics.

S'mores are toasted marshmallows with chocolate between two pieces of cracker.

Fireside nights

On some evenings, Lily's family sits around a fire outdoors. They chat, cook hot dogs, and make s'mores.

Lily's family

Lily lives with her parents and younger siblings on her grandparents' farm. Every Sunday, they go to church, where Lily sings in the choir.

Signature

Lily

How I say hello

Hi
Pronounced "hi"

Where I live

The family lives in the small town of Carrollton, Ohio, in the Midwestern USA.

Tara mother

Ridge brother

Anna sister

Jeff grandfather

Lily

Jason father

Marcella grandmother

Life on the farm

Lily loves living on a farm because she can climb trees and go on nature walks. She also likes living next door to her grandparents.

Andrea

Andrea is seven years old and comes from South Carolina. Andrea loves being a cheerleader. She practices with her squad twice a week, and they perform impressive routines at her school's football games. She also takes part in gymnastics. Her specialty is tumbling, which involves tricky somersaults.

This is the uniform Andrea wears when she is cheerleading.

Kim grandmother

Ebonie mother

Andrea

"I can't wait for my little baby brother to arrive."

At home

Andrea loves her house because it is close to her grandmother's. She has her own bedroom, although her dog, Klaus, likes to share it. Andrea's mom, Ebonie, is expecting a baby boy.

Andrea's house

Signature

Andrea

How I say hello

Hello
Pronounced "he-LO"

Where I live

South Carolina is in the Southern USA.

Ribs

Southern food

Andrea eats lots of tasty Southern food, such as ribs and grits. Grits are made from boiled, ground corn and are often eaten for breakfast with shrimp or bacon.

Grits with shrimp

Charlotte

Andrea lives in a town called Fort Mill in South Carolina, but goes to school just over the border in Charlotte, North Carolina.

Getting creative

Andrea's mother's hobby is art and she likes to share her passion with her daughter.

10

Joaquin practices the trombone every night after dinner.

Joaquin

Eleven-year-old Joaquin hails from the state of New Jersey. It is nicknamed the "Garden State" because much of it used to be farmland. He plays the trombone in his school band and performs in concerts twice a year. Both of Joaquin's parents speak Spanish fluently, and he can understand it pretty well.

Jared father

Stephanie mother

Natalia sister

Joaquin

Family life

Joaquin lives with his parents and his eight-year-old sister, Natalia. His mother's parents live nearby, and his grandmother takes him to school every day.

Joaquin's home

Favorite food

Joaquin absolutely loves bacon! His family also likes to eat traditional American food such as pizzas and hamburgers. In the summer, they sometimes barbecue outside on a grill.

Bacon and egg muffin

Signature

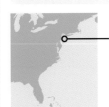

How I say hello

Hello
Pronounced "he-LO"

Where I live

New Jersey is located on the East Coast of the USA.

New York

Joaquin lives close to New York City, the most populated city in the USA. It contains more than 8 million inhabitants.

"I love history, especially learning about wars."

History crazy

Joaquin is interested in the past and spends his free time playing with toy soldiers or reading history books. When he's older, he'd like to be a history teacher or a paleontologist (someone who digs up fossils).

Cymian

Ten-year-old Cymian lives in Montana. Cymian is Native American, and he and his family are closely associated with the Shawnee tribe. Only about two percent of the US population is Native American, so keeping Native traditions alive is very important to Cymian's family. They are members of the Native American Church and live on a Native American reservation.

Mossy Creek sister **D'Arcy** mother **Joseph** father
Marj grandmother **Mitchell** brother **Cymian**

Meet the family

Cymian has an older sister, Mossy Creek, and a younger brother, Mitchell. They live with their parents, Joseph and D'Arcy, who are both students at Salish Kootenai College. The children often spend time with their grandmother, Marj.

Cymian's home

Cymian's family lives in a house on the grounds of the college. When Cymian's parents finish their studies, the family will move to a new home.

Native American food

The family often eats traditional Shawnee food, such as corn soup, and every family member helps with the cooking. Cymian also enjoys other food, such as macaroni, steak, and pizza.

Native Americans traditionally used a bow and arrow to hunt animals. ·····

Spooky fun

Halloween is Cymian's favorite time of year. He goes trick-or-treating with his friends and always gets a lot of candy!

The children's traditional clothes were made by their mother, D'Arcy.

Drumming with Dad

Cymian is still learning about his Native American culture. His dad has been teaching him to play the drum, so when Joseph sings in church Cymian can accompany him. In the future, Cymian may also join in special dances and ceremonies.

"I like to drum for my dad while he sings."

Feather fans are waved during dances.

Signature

Cymian

How I say hello

Hello
Pronounced "he-LO"

Where I live

Montana is in the Western USA.

Family tepee

Cymian's family keeps a tepee in the backyard. Tepees are tents made of cloth or animal skins stretched around wooden poles.

Baseball star

Cymian is an avid baseball player. He plays on the Ronan Scissortail team, which is coached by his dad. When he grows up, Cymian wants to play for a famous baseball team.

Alonso

Alonso is nine years old and lives in a town in the south of Mexico. The Mexican landscape is varied, with deserts in the north and mountainous jungles in the south. Alonso enjoys hiking in the mountains with his scout group and taking photographs of his adventures. Alonso's family believes that all people should be treated as equals, regardless of where they are from or what they believe.

Alonso in his scout uniform

Amanda
Aurora's wife

Aurora
sister

Luis
father

Liliana
mother

Javier
brother

Pánfilo

Alonso

Family

Alonso lives with his parents, Luis and Liliana, and his six-year-old brother, Javier. His older sister, Aurora, and her wife, Amanda, also live with them. The family's pet dog is named Pánfilo.

Chilis stuffed with meat and spices

Walnut cream

Pomegranate seeds

Chilis en nogada

Liliana cooking dinner

Mexican food

Liliana cooks most of the food for Alonso's family, including local specialties such as *chiles en nogada* and chicken with *mole negro*, which is a chili and chocolate sauce. Alonso likes to help his mom cook.

Toasted seeds mixed with honey and sugar inside a wafer

Alegrías

14

Celebrating

Alonso and his family celebrate the Mexican festival *Día de Muertos* (Day of the Dead). It takes place on November 1 and 2 every year. It is a cheerful festival when people honor their dead relatives with special food and decorate their homes with candles, flowers, and candy skulls.

Home

Alonso lives in a tall apartment building that has three towers and 180 apartments. He likes where he lives because there is a swimming pool and a forest nearby.

These skulls are made of sugar and are usually just for decoration.

"I love my computer and everything related to technology."

Alonso's PlayStation

Telling stories

Alonso is a very creative person. He likes to invent stories and then draw pictures to go with them. They are a great way of sharing his thoughts and feelings. He is thinking about becoming a painter when he's older, or perhaps an actor.

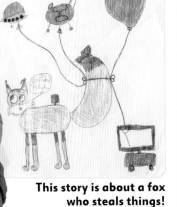

This story is about a fox who steals things!

Signature

How I say hello

Hola
Pronounced "oh-LAH"

Where I live

Alonso lives in a town called Huixquilucan, near Mexico City.

Alonso drawing

School

Alonso attends a Montessori school, which is a type of school that encourages children to choose what they want to learn each day. Lessons are often very hands-on and exciting.

Huixquilucan

Parts of the town where Alonso lives contain lots of houses built very close to each other.

South America

South America is a continent of natural wonders, ancient ruins, and bustling modern cities. Along its western side runs the longest mountain range in the world, the Andes, and in its heart lies the Amazon rain forest, home to millions of species of animal.

Darwin's frog

This frog is named after the famous naturalist Charles Darwin, who discovered it when traveling through Chile.

Angel Falls

Jutting out of the Venezuelan jungle, Angel Falls is the highest waterfall in the world. It is more than twice the height of the Empire State Building in New York City!

Ceviche

This popular seafood dish is made by pickling raw fish in the juice of lemons or limes.

Machu Picchu

Built by the Incas more than 500 years ago, the city of Machu Picchu lay hidden in the Andes until it was discovered by explorers in 1911.

Life in the Andes

The people of the Andes traditionally wear bright and colorful clothes. They also look after animals called alpacas.

Venezuela

Guyana

Ecuador

Galápagos Islands
(Ecuador)

Venezuela

Guyana

Colombia

Ecuador

○ **Suriname**
○ French Guiana
(France)

Suriname

Peru

Brazil

Colombia
Find Miguel on pages 22–23

Peru

Bolivia

Chile

Paraguay

Brazil

Argentina

Uruguay

Chile

Brazil
Find Rafael on pages 18–19

Argentina

Argentina
Find Trini on pages 20–21

Bolivia

Falkland Islands
(United Kingdom)

Uruguay

Paraguay

Rafael

Rafael is nine years old and lives in Brazil, which is the largest country in South America. The people in Brazil speak Portuguese. Rafael has many hobbies, including playing the keyboard and inventing his own country! Like many Brazilians, Rafael loves soccer, but his true passion is skateboarding.

Carlos Alberto grandfather

Mauricio father

Silvia mother

Celina grandmother

Rafael

Renato grandfather

City home

Rafael lives in Rio de Janeiro, the second-largest city in Brazil. His home is in the south of the city, and it has great views of the mountains surrounding Rio.

Family life

Rafael lives with his parents, Silvia and Mauricio. He is also very close to his grandparents. Three of them live in Rio, too. Rafael's other grandmother lives in a different part of Brazil, but he visits her often.

Signature

How I say hello

Olá
Pronounced "olla"

Where I live

Rio is in the southeast of Brazil.

Kaki

Feijoada

Favorite food

Rafael loves to eat pasta and Japanese food, and his favorite fruit is the *kaki*, or Japanese persimmon. Rafael's nanny, Solange, often makes *feijoada*, which is a traditional black-bean stew with pork.

Wonder of the World

One of Rio's most famous sights is a statue of Jesus Christ, which overlooks the city. In 2007, it was named as one of the "New Seven Wonders of the World."

Fluffy friend

Rafael has one pet, a friendly rabbit named Lino. Lino likes to play indoors with Rafael and eat carrots.

Carnival costume

The Rio Carnival is a famous celebration that takes place every year. Rafael and his friends like to dress up to watch the carnival dancers parade through the streets.

Schoolbook

Rafael spends his mornings doing homework and then goes to school in the afternoon. He also has extra classes in music, art, and English.

Rafael's skateboard is one of his favorite things.

Made-up country

Rafael loves inventing his own games. He's even created his own country, Frankinópolis, with its own language, transportation system, and detailed maps, which are drawn by Rafael.

"I love to play many instruments, but I'm best at playing the keyboard."

Family band

Each family member plays an instrument. Dad bangs the drums, Mom strums the guitar and sings, and Rafael plays the keyboard.

Trini

" When I grow up I want to be president of Argentina because I would like to end poverty."

Ten-year-old Trini comes from Argentina, a country famous for the tango, soccer, and its delicious steak. Trini is incredibly active, and when she's not dancing or singing at her local academy, she can be found playing tennis or swimming. She is also learning how to play golf, and heads to the course on Sundays to play a round with her dad.

Flavio
father

Carolina
mother

Sofia
sister

··· Golf clubs

Delfina
sister

Trini

The family

Trini is the oldest child in her house. Her younger sisters are seven-year-old Delfina and Sofia, who is just three. The sisters love to watch movies together. Trini's mother, Carolina, is a fashion designer, while her dad, Flavio, works in a bank.

Life in the suburbs

Trini's home is situated in Buenos Aires, the capital of Argentina. Trini likes her neighborhood because it is so small that she never gets lost! In the summer, the family goes to Córdoba Province, in the center of the country, where they ride horses through a landscape of beautiful rivers and mountains.

Time to learn

Every morning Trini is driven to school. It is only a short ride—about three blocks—and when she is older she wants to cycle there by herself. If Trini could change anything in the world she would make students spend more time outside and less time sitting at their desks!

Reyes Magos

Trini and her family don't exchange presents on Christmas Day, but a few days later, on January 6. This day, called *Reyes Magos* (Three Wise Men) is a tradition in many Latin American countries.

Trini's church

Religious beliefs

Trini's family is Catholic, and they go to church to worship every Sunday. Trini is about to take part in an important tradition called First Communion. Together with her mother, she designed a beautiful white dress for the occasion.

Trini's First Communion dress

Argentinian classics

Every Sunday, Flavio fires up the barbeque and grills different types of meat. The dish of meats is called an *asado*, and it is a traditional meal of the region. Sometimes the family drinks *mate* alongside it. This is a hot drink made from dried leaves and drunk through a silver straw. For breakfast, the sisters are sometimes treated to a caramel-like spread called *dulce de leche*.

Mate

Dulce de leche

Flavio's *asado*

Signature

Trinidad

How I say hello

Hola
Pronounced "OH-la"

Where I live

Buenos Aires is located on the east coast of Argentina.

Buenos Aires

The capital of Argentina is a bustling modern city. It attracts thousands of tourists every year, who are eager to see its restaurants, shops, and European-style architecture.

Miguel

Buenas
Pronounced "BWEN-ASS"

Where I live

Colombia is in northwest South America.

Monteria
Monteria is situated alongside the Sinú River in northern Colombia. The town's main business is cattle farming.

Miguel

Miguel lives in Colombia in South America. Colombia is a very hot country and in Miguel's town, Monteria, the average temperature is 95°F (35°C). Monteria is famous for a special hat, the *Sombrero Vueltiao*, which was traditionally worn by ranchers to protect them from the sun. On special occasions, such as his town's saint's day, Miguel wears the hat, a checkered shirt, and a neck tie.

Miguel's home
Nine-year-old Miguel lives in a one-story house with his parents, sister, and grandmother. The family is Catholic, and they go to church every Sunday.

The *Sombrero Vueltiao* is also the national symbol of Colombia.

Traditional food
Fried fish with coconut rice and plantain (a type of savory banana) is a popular local dish in Monteria. However, Miguel's favorite food is chicken and fries!

Fried plantain slices are known as *patacones*.

The fish has the skin and head left on.

Coconut rice is sweet and sticky.

Chopped avocado

"I want a games console because I like video games a lot."

Favorite things
Miguel has a pet cat, named Sisi, that he loves very much. He is passionate about soccer, and when he grows up he wants to be a superstar goalkeeper. Miguel also loves to dance and sing to Colombian coastal folk music called *champeta*.

Family time

Miguel has a very close family. His grandmother on his mother's side, Yanila, lives with him. She cooks all the family's meals and takes care of him when his parents are at work. Every Sunday, Miguel's whole family gathers at his other grandmother's house for a big lunch.

Laura cousin
Lina sister
Ema mother
José cousin
Sebastian cousin

Jesus cousin
Miguel
Laura cousin

Miguel's schoolbook

REVISTA DE LOS ALIMENTOS

Classroom

Toy collection

Miguel is very proud of his toy car collection. He also collects action figures.

School life

Miguel spends his mornings doing chores with his sister and goes to school in the afternoon. Miguel is a member of his class soccer team. When his team took part in the school tournament, they came in second.

Traditional sandals

Iguana alert!

Miguel enjoys going to the park with his friends. If they look closely, they can usually spot iguanas (a type of lizard) snacking on fruit or leaves.

Europe

Europe is a continent of contrasts, where modern skyscrapers stand alongside buildings from the time of the ancient Greeks and Romans. In the far north, there is little sunlight in the winter, while in the east, European traditions mix with those of Asia.

The Colosseum

The ruins of this ancient stadium in Rome, Italy, are a reminder of its famous past, when gladiators fought to entertain people.

Blue tit

This small bird can be heard singing its heart out in yards throughout Europe.

Fjords

Along the coast of Norway lie more than a thousand breathtaking fjords. These deep channels of water were created by glaciers during the last Ice Age.

Goulash

This warm stew is a popular meal in Central European countries, such as Hungary.

Celebrating diversity

In most inner-city schools in Europe you will find children whose families come from a wide range of different countries.

FACT FILE

Europe borders Asia to the east, while Africa lies to the south.

Population

715 million

Number of countries

47

Biggest city

Moscow, in Russia, is the largest city completely in Europe. More than 12 million people live there.

Longest river

The Volga River in Russia flows for 2,293 miles (3,690 km) before it reaches the Caspian Sea.

Highest mountain

Russia's Mount Elbrus is 18,510 ft (5,642 m) tall.

Ireland
Find Jack on page 27

Germany
Find Clara on pages 34–35

Sweden
Find Stella on page 36

Finland
Find Mattus on page 28

Russia
Find Yaroslav on page 37

France
Find Morgan on page 31

France
Find Solal on page 30

Hungary

Turkey

Italy

Iceland

Spain
Find Lucas on page 33

United Kingdom
Find Alec on page 26

Croatia

Greece
Find Maria on page 32

Poland
Find Martyna on page 29

Iceland

Sweden

Norway

Finland

Russia

Estonia

Latvia

Lithuania

Denmark

Russia

Netherlands

United Kingdom

Ireland

Belgium

Luxembourg

Germany

Poland

Belarus

Czech Republic

Ukraine

Slovakia

Liechtenstein

France

Austria

Hungary

Switzerland

Portugal

Italy

Croatia

Romania

Moldova

San Marino

Serbia

Spain

Andorra

Kosovo

Bulgaria

Macedonia

Turkey

Vatican City

Slovenia

Greece

Malta

Bosnia and Herzegovina

Albania

Montenegro

Alec

Sabina
sister

Mark
father

Eliza
mother

Lucek

Alec

Seven-year-old Alec lives in the historic city of Winchester in England. His dad is English, while his mom is from Poland in Eastern Europe. Alec speaks Polish with his mother, but English with his friends. One of Alec's favorite things to do is to go for chocolate ice cream in the city center.

Mushroom and meat *pierogi*

Alec's home

Home life

Alec lives with his parents and baby sister, Sabina, in a yellow house. In his spare time, Alec takes his pet dog, Lucek, to the park.

Grandma's cooking

When Alec's Polish grandmother visits, she makes *pierogi*, which are traditional Polish dumplings.

> "When I grow up I want to be a policeman and catch robbers."

Best friends

Hugh is Alec's closest friend. Hugh's family is from the Philippines, in Southeast Asia. Hugh and Alec love to make cool things out of LEGO together.

Alec and Hugh play together after school.

King Alfred

A statue of this famous English king stands in the center of Winchester.

Jack

Jack lives on a working farm in Ireland, a country off the coast of mainland Europe. Jack loves dinosaurs and wishes more than anything that they still roamed the Earth! At school, he plays Gaelic football, a traditional Irish ball game.

Jack in his Gaelic football uniform. He plays every spring.

Joseph father
Pamela mother
Kate sister
Anthony brother
Jack
Emma sister
Ciara sister

Farmhouse

Family farm

Jack and his family live in the countryside. Jack is the oldest child and has four younger siblings—two sets of twins! Kate and Emma are six, while Ciara and Anthony are four.

Irish stew

Jack's family loves stew, a mixture of meat and vegetables that are cooked together and served with mashed potatoes. In the spring, the family sometimes eats lamb from the farm.

Signature

How I say hello

Hello
Pronounced "he-LO"

Where I live

Jack lives in Kilbeggan, a town in the heart of Ireland.

Feeding the cattle

On the weekends and during school breaks, Jack looks after the animals on the farm with his dad, brother, and grandad. When he grows up he wants to be a farmer.

Mattus

> "When I grow up I would like to direct movies."

Mattus is eight years old and lives in Helsinki, Finland. He is always busy and enjoys activities such as basketball and street dancing. In winter, he sometimes plays ice hockey at school, while at home he practices the piano. Mattus's favorite time of year is summer, when the weather is warm and he doesn't have to go to school!

Home life

Mattus's apartment

Mattus and his family live in an apartment. Lots of his friends also live in their building so there is always someone to play with.

Signature

Panu
father

Mona
mother

Mattus

Eeve
sister

Mattus

How I say hello

Hei
Pronounced "hay"

Where I live

Helsinki is the capital city of Finland.

Helsinki

Helsinki is a busy seaside city. Mattus loves to visit the local amusement park, Linnanmäki.

Liver casserole

Mattus likes to eat liver casserole. It is made of rice, ground liver, butter, syrup, eggs, and onions.

Freestyler

Mattus performs in a street dance group and practices for five hours a week. Last year, they won the gold medal at the Finnish national children's competition.

Mattus's ice hockey stick

Martyna

Marcin father

Katarzyna mother

Martyna

Malwina sister

Ten-year-old Martyna lives in the countryside near Gdańsk, Poland. She enjoys the peace and quiet of her home and likes playing outside in the garden. Martyna is learning how to play the guitar and spends lots of time practicing at home and at school. When she finishes school she would love to visit Paris or New York.

How I say hello

Cześć
Pronounced "chesh-ch"

Where I live

Gdańsk is pronounced "dansk."

Gdańsk
Gdańsk is over a thousand years old. It is on the coast of Poland.

My family

Martyna lives with her sister, who is five years old, and her parents, who are both engineers. They swim and cycle together on the weekend.

Martyna's house

Martyna enjoys playing the guitar and also loves to sing.

Czerwone buraczki (beet salad)

Golabki (ground beef cabbage rolls in tomato sauce)

Kotlety mielone (meatballs)

Dinner time

Dumplings and meat are often on the menu in Martyna's home. However, her favorite foods are homegrown vegetables and pancakes.

Wrapped up warm

Martyna and her sister, Malwina, like to go skiing. To keep warm and safe they wear special ski clothes.

Solal

Lila
sister

Sabrina
mother

Anthony
father

Sacha
brother

Solal

Apple

Solal comes from Nancy, a town in northeastern France. His favorite thing to do is visit the park, where he can ride his scooter or go on the slides. When it's sunny, Solal heads to a large square in Nancy, called Place Stanislas, and drinks a pomegranate-flavored drink called grenadine.

"When I grow up, I want to be an architect. I love drawing house plans."

At home

Seven-year-old Solal lives with his parents and older siblings, Lila and Sacha. Every night, Solal goes to bed early so he doesn't fall asleep in class the next day!

Solal's home

Quiche lorraine

Solal often eats the region's specialty, quiche lorraine. It's a pie made of eggs and bacon that tastes great hot or cold.

Signature

Solal

How I say hello

Bonjour
Pronounced "bon-JHOOR"

Where I live

France is a country in Western Europe.

Favorite park

Solal likes to play in Parc de la Pépinière, which is a beautiful park in the middle of Nancy.

Playing chess

Chess is a popular pastime in France. It's a board game, invented in India a long time ago, that requires a lot of skill and concentration. Solal likes to try to beat his older brother, Sacha.

Morgan

Morgan is nine years old and lives in Lyon, a large city in France that was originally founded by the Romans. He likes to ride his bike and also has a yellow belt in judo. Morgan's favorite time of year is fall, because he loves looking at the changing colors of the leaves.

Tasty lasagne

Morgan loves eating cheese and fish, but his favorite meal is lasagne, an Italian dish made of sheets of pasta, ground beef, sauce, and cheese.

Mom's apartment building

Home life

Morgan splits his time between his mother, Pelagie, who has an apartment near the Rhône, a big river, and his father, Eric, who lives about 3 miles (5 km) away.

Pelagie mother

Eric father

Morgan

Signature

Morgan

How I say hello

Bonjour
Pronounced "bon-JHOOR"

Where I live

Lyon is only a short drive from the Alps mountains.

Lyon
Located on the banks of two rivers, Lyon has always been a busy city with many industries.

Morgan enjoys playing with his cars.

Playtime

In his spare time, Morgan loves playing with his toy cars and LEGO. In the playground at school, his friends and he often play a French version of tag, called *loup touche touche.*

Maria

Artemis
mother **Lefteris**
father

Markos
brother **Maria**

Maria is eight years old and lives in Athens, the capital city of Greece. Maria loves nature and whenever possible she and her family go on trips to explore the nearby mountains. Maria likes to go to the park with her friends—they play hide and seek and have competitions to see who is the fastest on the monkey bars.

···· Maria is learning magic tricks.

" I wish I could perform magic tricks. I love watching magicians do them! "

Maria's home

Family and home

Maria lives with her mom, dad, and younger brother, Markos. They have a nanny named Voula who looks after them when their parents are at work.

How I say hello

Yiassas
Pronounced "YA-sass"

Plant power

Maria wants to learn how to grow and look after plants so that she can set up her own plant nursery when she is older.

Where I live

Greece is in southeastern Europe and has coasts on the Mediterranean Sea.

········ Tomato

Greek salad

········ Green bell pepper

Feta cheese ······

Athens
The Ancient Greeks built many impressive temples, such as the Parthenon in Athens.

Grilled fish

Fresh food

In Greece, people use lots of fresh ingredients to make meals. Maria enjoys cooking and helps her dad prepare meals, such as grilled fish or Greek salad.

Lucas

Lucas is six years old and lives with his family in the Spanish city of Barcelona. When he grows up, Lucas wants to be a professional soccer player, and he practices with his team twice a week. Lucas also enjoys fishing, and his parents take him to the local river once a month to try to catch fresh fish for their dinner!

Signature

Lucas

How I say hello

Hola
Pronounced "oh-la"

Where I live

Barcelona is the capital city of Catalonia, a region in northeastern Spain.

Barcelona
Barcelona is known for the Sagrada Familia church, designed by Antoni Gaudí.

Maria
mother

Jonathan
father

Carlota
sister

Lucas

Home life
Lucas and his family live in a house near the coast. They all enjoy swimming and even have a pool in their backyard.

Lucas's house

Family dinner
On special occasions Lucas's grandmother, Conchita, makes paella— a traditional Spanish seafood and rice dish.

Paella

Baturro wear
Lucas and Carlota wear traditional Baturro clothing during festivals. The clothes are from their mother's hometown of Zaragoza and are similar to what people wore 150 years ago.

Lucas is wearing his youth team's soccer uniform.

Clara

Nine-year-old Clara lives in a small village in Germany, the seventh-largest country in Europe. Germany is where the tradition of the Christmas tree comes from, and Christmas is Clara's favorite time of year! During the festive season, her father bakes a traditional German cake called stollen, and her great-grandfather carves amazing wooden decorations.

Andreas
father

Kathrin
mother

Stephan
brother

Clara

Brand new home

Clara's new family home is being decorated. Her father is renovating the inside and her mother is making furniture. Clara helps her parents with their projects whenever she can.

Meet the family

Clara lives with her parents, Andreas and Kathrin, who are both bakers, and her 13-year-old brother, Stephan. The family also has a pet cat named Elvis.

Wickelklöse with red cabbage, mushrooms, chives, and pork

What they eat

Clara and her family love to eat special savory potato dumplings called *Wickelklöse*. Clara also likes roast chicken, pasta, and ice cream.

Christmas carving

Clara's great-grandfather is a wood carver. He creates tall, detailed carvings called Christmas pyramids.

Clara likes to wear colorful leggings.

How I say hello

Hallo
Pronounced "ha-LOH"

Where I live

Vielau is in the eastern part of Germany.

Countryside living

Clara's village, Vielau, is in the hilly green region of Saxony. Her family spends as much time as possible outdoors, hiking, swimming in the lake, or growing vegetables in their backyard.

Hobbies

Clara loves horseback riding and dreams of having her own horse one day. She also likes playing with friends, especially hide and seek, and driving go-karts!

777th Anniversary

In 2015, Vielau celebrated its 777th birthday! The whole village was decorated with dolls, flags, and bunting, and everyone had a big party.

Collecting plants

Clara attends elementary school and she loves it so much that she never wants to leave. She is very proud of her recent nature project, which involved collecting and pressing flowers inside a book.

This is a daisy that Clara picked and then pressed.

"I want to work with animals when I grow up."

Signature

Stella

How I say hello

Hej
Pronounced "hay"

Where I live

Sweden is part of a region of Europe known as Scandinavia.

Stockholm

Stella lives near Sweden's capital city, Stockholm. The city is spread across 14 islands, and more than 30 percent of Stockholm is made up of waterways.

Out and about

Stella's family loves doing things outdoors. They swim in the summer when it's warm, and ski in the winter when there is a lot of snow. Her mother likes sailing in their small dinghy, but Stella isn't a big fan. She prefers trampolining in her backyard!

Stella is eight years old and lives in Sweden in the far north of Europe. She enjoys school and her favorite subjects are math and music. Outside of school Stella is also very busy, spending her time playing the piano, dancing, and climbing.

Stella likes to choose her own outfit every morning.

Jens father

Charlotte mother

Stella

Jacob brother

Family home

Stella lives in a two-story house with her parents and younger brother, Jacob, in Täby, near Stockholm. Her house is a 15-minute walk from her school and her best friend, Amanda, lives next door.

Stella's house

Top chef

Stella's favorite TV program is a children's cooking show. It has inspired her to start cooking with her family.

Cooking with Mom and Jacob

Swedish meatballs with lingonberry jam

Yaroslav made a family portrait from LEGO. This is him!

Yaroslav

Eight-year-old Yaroslav lives in the Russian city of Moscow. His favorite season is summer, because it's warm and he can spend a lot of time outdoors. He loves to travel to Odessa in neighboring Ukraine to go to the beach.

Signature

How I say hello

Privyet
Pronounced "pree-VYET"

Where I live

Russia is the world's largest country. Different parts of it are in Europe and Asia.

Moscow
Moscow is in the European part of Russia. Famous landmarks include Red Square, the Kremlin, and St. Basil's Cathedral.

Yaroslav's apartment building

Erik
brother

Vitaliy
father

Natalia
mother

Yaroslav

Home life
Yaroslav and his family live in an apartment building. Yaroslav's favorite place is the attic, where he can keep his toys safe from his baby brother!

Making robots
Yaroslav is passionate about making and building things, either with LEGO or using a computer. He has already built his own robot and would like to be a computer programmer when he is older.

"I wish Erik would stay a baby forever (but become a little smarter)."

37

Africa

Africa is a huge continent spanning cities, deserts, rain forests, and wild grasslands. It is home to thousands of tribes of people who speak about 2,000 different languages. Africa is the hottest continent, and it contains the world's largest desert, the Sahara, which is nearly as big as the US.

Fresh produce
A variety of fruit and vegetables are grown in Africa, such as the African horned cucumber.

Ancient wonder
There were Seven Wonders of the Ancient World, consisting of the most impressive human constructions. Today, only one remains—the Great Pyramid of Giza in Egypt (seen here in the center).

Longest river
The Nile is the longest river in the world. Including its tributaries, it runs through 11 countries.

Vast rain forests
Africa has millions of miles of tropical rain forests. They are home to more than 8,000 different types of plant.

Tallest mountain
Mount Kilimanjaro is 19,341 ft (5,895 m) high and located in Tanzania in East Africa.

Wildlife
Africa is famous for its wildlife. It is home to lions, elephants, crocodiles, cheetahs, and more animals!

Walking to school
Many children who live in remote villages walk to school. Some must walk a very long way, even when it is hot or raining.

Morocco
Find Bassma on page 40

Algeria

Libya

Ethiopia
Find Yohanna on page 41

Tanzania
Find Shigo on pages 42-43

Tunisia

Morocco

Algeria

Libya

Egypt

Canary Islands
(Spain)

Western
Sahara

Cape
Verde

Mauritania

Mali

Niger

Chad

Sudan

Eritrea

Senegal

Djibouti

Gambia

Guinea-Bissau

Guinea

Burkina
Faso

Nigeria

Central
African
Republic

South
Sudan

Ethiopia

Sierra Leone

Ivory
Coast

Liberia

Ghana

Togo

Benin

Equatorial
Guinea

São Tomé
and Príncipe

Cameroon

Gabon

Congo

Democratic
Republic
of the Congo

Somalia

Uganda

Rwanda
Burundi

Kenya

Egypt

Kenya

Nigeria

Tanzania

Seychelles

Chad

Angola

Zambia

Malawi

Comoros

Mozambique

Madagascar

Mauritius

Réunion (France)

Namibia

Zimbabwe

Botswana

Swaziland

Lesotho

South
Africa

Ghana
Find Jedidiah on page 46

Botswana
Find Joshua on pages 44-45

Ghana

Namibia

Rwanda

South Africa
Find Amu on pages 48-49

South Africa
Find Hafsa on page 47

Bassma

"My brother Mohammed Amine always makes me laugh."

Bassma is eight years old and lives in a small, rural village in central Morocco. Her family is Berber—an ancient group of people from North Africa. Bassma speaks a Berber language known as Tashelhit, but she also knows some French and Arabic. Bassma and her family are Muslim, and Bassma enjoys going to the mosque to pray.

Bassma

Zaina
mother

Lahcen
father

Merouane
brother

Mohammed Amine
brother

Family life

Bassma and her family live in a small house. They share a yard with some of their family members who live next door. Bassma always has lots of cousins around for her to play with.

Bassma at home

Signature

Bassma

How I say hello

Azul
Pronounced "ah-zool"

Where I live

Bassma lives about 60 miles (100 km) from Marrakech, Morocco's fourth-largest city.

Local food

Bassma's favorite food is couscous, a traditional Berber dish made with durum wheat. It is often served with a meat or vegetable stew called a tagine.

... Couscous

.... Goat tagine

Marrakech

Built by the Berbers, Marrakech's old city, or *medina*, is famous for its red walls and busy markets, which are called *souks*.

Bassma often wears long skirts. For special events, she wears a dress called a kaftan.

Yohanna

Seven-year-old Yohanna lives in Addis Ababa, the capital of Ethiopia. It is the fourth-largest city in Africa. Yohanna's two favorite places to visit are the Edna shopping mall and the Lion Zoo.

Bitania
sister

Beza
mother

Tesfa
father

Abemelek
brother

Yohanna

Yohanna likes to wear brightly colored clothes.

Yohanna on the porch of her home

Family

Yohanna lives with her mother, a teacher, her father, an aircraft technician, and her two younger siblings. Yohanna's family is Christian.

Favorite food

Yohanna's family often eats *wat*, which is an Ethiopian stew. They serve it with roasted lamb, rice, and a flatbread called *injera*.

Shiro wat (pea and lentil stew)

Injera

Bread

Doro wat (chicken stew)

Rice

Roasted lamb

Signature

Yohanna

How I say hello

Tadiyass
Pronounced "ta-DEE-yas"

Where I live

Addis Ababa is in the center of Ethiopia.

Addis Ababa

Located at the foot of Mount Entoto, Addis Ababa is the fifth-highest capital city in the world.

Playtime

When she's not at school, Yohanna likes to play jump-roping games with her friends. She also enjoys playing soccer with her brother, Abemelek.

Shigo

Sopa
Pronounced "sop-ah"

Where I live

Shigo lives in a village called Tungamalenga in the Iringa region of Tanzania.

Shigo

Shigo lives in Tanzania in East Africa. She is seven years old and a member of the Maasai people. The Maasai live in northern Tanzania and parts of neighboring Kenya. Owning and raising cattle is an important part of the Maasai way of life. Shigo's family also owns goats and sheep.

Like most Maasai, sister Namnyaki wears brightly colored clothes.

National park

Tungamalenga is just outside the Ruaha National Park, which is the largest wildlife park in Tanzania.

Brick house

Shigo's family lives in a brick house with a metal roof. Brick homes are better at keeping people warm at night than the more traditional mud huts.

Goat meat with onions

Ugali

Maasai food

Most days, Shigo eats *ugali*, which is made from corn flour and similar to porridge. Shigo's favorite food is meat, especially goat and beef.

Nehatibu
mother

Matambile
father

Elizabeti
Matambile's second wife

Meet the family

Shigo's father, Matambile, has two wives and 10 children. Shigo lives with her parents, her father's second wife, and her brothers and sisters.

Helping out

Raising animals is hard work, and Shigo helps out whenever she can. She often milks the cows with her mother.

"I wish I had a car to drive all the children to school, so our books wouldn't get wet in the rainy season."

Sister Rabeka wears a homemade beaded necklace.

Shigo wears shoes to walk to school.

Going to school

Every day, Shigo walks to school, even during the rainy season, which lasts from December to May. She really enjoys school and would like to become a teacher when she is older.

Playing netball

Shigo's school

Making jewelry

Shigo and her sisters are learning to make bead jewelry with their mothers. Maasai people can tell where other Maasai are from by looking at the colors and designs of their jewelry.

Learning a craft

This collarlike necklace is made of thousands of tiny beads.

Necklace

Beaded pendant

Working pet

Shigo's family owns several dogs, which help to guard the cattle. The dogs keep the livestock safe from lions or people who steal animals.

Joshua

Eight-year-old Joshua lives in the Kalahari Desert, a huge sandy area that covers about two-thirds of his home country, Botswana. Joshua and his family are members of the San tribe, and they earn a living by making and selling traditional crafts, such as jewelry. Life in the desert is hard, especially during the dry season, when hardly any rain falls.

Desert home

Joshua and his family live in a house made of cow dung and corrugated iron, with no electricity. They are saving up to buy bricks and cement to build a new house.

The family home

Nicodemus
father

Elizabeth
sister

Tumku
mother

Moses
cousin

Judas
brother

Duncan
cousin

Joshua

Joshua's family

Joshua lives with his parents and his older brother and sister. His cousins Duncan and Moses also live with him. The family is Christian. They attend church every Sunday and Joshua's parents sing in the choir.

Joshua's school uniform was donated by a local diamond mining company. ·········

Playing music

Joshua loves music and has even invented his own musical instrument! It is made of tin and string tied to a tree, and Joshua often performs songs for his family and friends.

Signature

Joshua

How I say hello

Dumela
Pronounced "do-MEL-ah"

Where I live

Botswana has no coastline. It is bordered by South Africa, Namibia, Zimbabwe, and Zambia.

D'kar

Joshua goes to school in the small village of D'kar. He walks there, even in the rainy season.

Traditional dance

Joshua's mother, Tumku, is teaching her children a traditional San dance. The San people use dance to try to heal sick people, celebrate a good hunt, or even to bring the rain. Dancers wear traditional outfits made from animal skins.

Jewelry the family made from pieces of ostrich egg

Family business

The family jewelry-making business does not always make a lot of money, so the family also searches the veld (land) for animals and plants to eat.

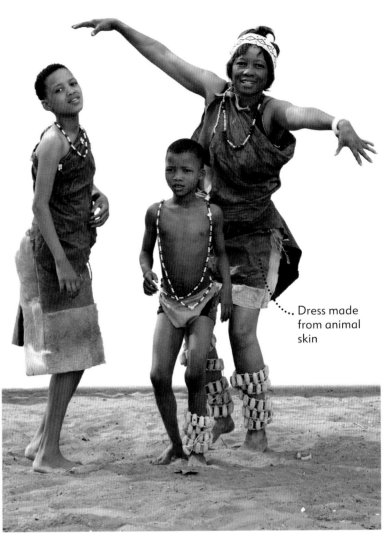

Dress made from animal skin

Story time

Joshua doesn't have a television or computer, but he still has access to some first-class entertainment, thanks to his grandmother. She is excellent at telling stories to the children.

"I love listening to my grandmother tell stories."

Horned melons

Local food

What Joshua eats depends on what his family finds out in the veld. During the dry season, horned melons are a valuable source of water. The family usually eats whatever they find with mealie-meal, a kind of porridge.

Eating lunch

45

Jedidiah

Seven-year-old Jedidiah lives in Ghana, West Africa. English is the official language in Ghana, but about 80 languages are spoken there. At home, he speaks the Twi language, but at school Jedidiah's classes are in English. He has many hobbies and his most recent one is drumming.

Family home

Jedidiah lives in a spacious house with his parents, two brothers, and adopted sister. The family is Catholic, and they spend every Saturday studying the Bible.

Signature

How I say hello

Maakye
Pronounced "maah-chee"

Where I live

Jedidiah lives in the Tema district on the south coast of Ghana.

Blessing sister
Sheila mother
Hamel brother
Melvin father
Abishua brother
Jedidiah

Ghanaian food

Jedidiah's family likes to eat healthy food, and they grow a lot of their own fruit and vegetables. One of their favorite meals is *agushi* and *kontomire* stews with plantain.

Plantain is like banana but with a savory taste.

Agushi stew contains crushed melon seeds.

Kontomire stew includes mashed taro leaves and fish.

Fontomfrom, or "talking drum"

Sakumono Township

Jedidiah's house is in Sakumono Township, a small, busy town next to a wetland in the Tema district.

Playtime

Jedidiah and Abishua enjoy playing *oware*, a traditional game very popular all over West Africa. The goal of the game is to capture your opponent's seeds.

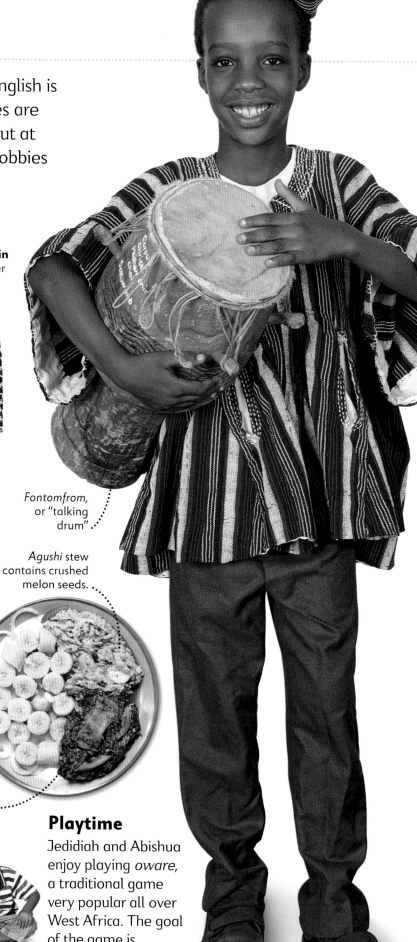

Hafsa

South African Hafsa is seven years old and lives in the city of Pretoria. Her family is Muslim, and Hafsa wears a brightly colored headscarf when she goes to her local mosque to pray. South Africa has 11 official languages and Hafsa speaks three of them—English, Ndebele, and Zulu.

"I love being in a big family because I have lots of cousins to play with. I'm never bored!"

This headscarf is also known as a hijab.

Budding ballerina
Hafsa enjoys dancing and has been learning ballet for about a year. She is also an avid runner.

Signature

HAFSA

How I say hello
Salibonani
Pronounced "sal-ee-bon-AR-NEE"

Where I live

Pretoria is one of South Africa's three capital cities. The other two are Cape Town and Bloemfontein.

Mpendulo
father

Muhammad-Ali
brother

Sahnun
brother

Hafsa

Luyanda
mother

Hafsa's home
Hafsa lives with her parents, brothers, grandmother, other relatives, and an old pet cat. Her father is a vegetable farmer and a hip-hop musician. Her mother helps companies sell their products online, and she is also a personal stylist.

National hero
This huge statue in Pretoria is of the famous former South African leader Nelson Mandela.

Growing vegetables
Hafsa's father grows a lot of the food that his family eats. Hafsa's grandmother raises chickens for their eggs and to eat.

Umgqushu

Cow-heel stew

Traditional food
Hafsa loves pizza, but the family mainly eats traditional South African food, such as *umgqushu*, which is beans with crushed corn kernels, and cow-heel stew.

47

Fikile
mother

Thandazo
sister

Amu

Mthokozisi
brother

Amu

Amukelani, or Amu to her friends, is a 10-year-old from South Africa. She lives with seven members of her family in a village called Msholozi in the northeast of the country. Amu's village is surrounded by beautiful countryside, so she loves to play outside—even when it's raining!

Happy family

Amu lives with her mother, Fikile, who is a nurse, her older sister, Thandazo, and her younger brother, Mthokozisi. Her grandmother, aunt, and two cousins also live with them. Amu and her family are Christian and go to church every Sunday.

Beef stew

Morogo (African spinach)

Tinkhobe (boiled corn)

Playing games

Amu was born with a condition called spina bifida, which affects her spine. It is hard for Amu to walk long distances, but she is still very active. She loves jumping rope, which is traditionally called *incantfu'u*. She often jumps rope with her sister and her cousin, Nowelthu.

Gladys cooking outside

Home cooking

Amu's grandmother, Gladys, cooks for the family. She prepares most of the meals inside the house, but some dishes, such as *tinkhobe*, are cooked outside.

Medal collection

Amu is very proud of her medals. Three of them are for sports—two for shot put and one for running. The other medals are for being the top achiever in her class, two years in a row.

Signature

Amukelani

How I say hello

Avuxeni

Pronounced "a-ve-shay-nee"

Where I live

South Africa is located at the bottom of Africa.

Nelspruit

Nelspruit is the closest city to Amu's village. It has more than 50,000 inhabitants and is located on the Crocodile River.

"I would like everyone to be able to afford food, shelter, and clothing."

Bath time

In the summer, bath time is outdoors. Amu's brother, Mthokozisi, and her cousin, Sinenkosi, love playing in the tub together.

Going shopping

Amu's family buys some of their food at the local supermarket and some in town. They also grow their own vegetables and keep chickens for eggs and meat.

...... Amu is wearing traditional Tsonga tribal clothes. She and her family are Tsonga people.

Amu's X-ray shows her spine with its special metal pins.

Amazing Amu

Amu's spina bifida means that she needs metal pins to support her spine. Amu's condition can be hard, but it has inspired her—she'd like to become a doctor when she's older so she can help other people like her.

Asia

Asia is a vast continent with a rich history. Originally famed for its delicious spices and ancient empires, today it is just as well-known for its high-tech gadgets and rapidly expanding cities. About 60 percent of the world's population lives in Asia.

Sushi
A delicacy in Japan, sushi is made of cooked rice and other ingredients, such as vegetables or seafood.

The Great Wall of China
This incredible monument is the largest in the world—including all branches, it is more than 12,500 miles (20,000 km) long. Some parts were built more than 2,000 years ago.

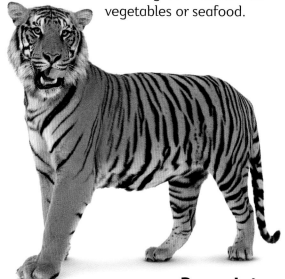

Bengal tiger
The forests of India and Bangladesh are home to the Bengal tiger. This fierce predator is at risk of becoming extinct due to hunting and the loss of its habitat.

Buddhist monks
Buddhism originated in India and is now a popular religion all over Asia. Buddhist monks are required to shave their heads.

Israel
Find Erel on page 66

Kazakhstan
Find Bolat on pages 64–65

Mongolia
Find Robert on pages 54–55

Nepal

Japan
Find Sotaro on pages 56–57

Bahrain
Find Khalifa on page 67

Iraq

Russia

Kazakhstan

Mongolia

Armenia **Georgia**
Azerbaijan
Turkey **Uzbekistan** **Kyrgyzstan**
Turkmenistan **Tajikistan**

North Korea

Cyprus **Syria**
Lebanon
Israel **Jordan** **Iraq** **Iran** **Afghanistan**
Kuwait
Bahrain **Pakistan**
Saudi Arabia **Oman**
Yemen
Qatar **United Arab Emirates**

South Korea
China **Japan**
Taiwan

South Korea
Find Yeh-Lin on pages 58–59

Nepal
India **Bhutan**
Bangladesh

Maldives **Sri Lanka** **Southeast Asia**
(see pages 70–75)

Pakistan
Find Murk on pages 62–63

Sri Lanka

India
Find Vishnu on page 61

China
Find Shaowei on pages 52–53

India
Find Mehak on page 60

Shaowei

Seven-year-old Shaowei lives in Beijing, the capital of China. Beijing is one of the biggest cities in the world. It has a population of more than 21 million people and is home to some of the world's most famous landmarks, including the Forbidden City. Shaowei has many hobbies, including yo-yoing, playing table tennis and soccer, and rock climbing.

Shaowei is wearing his school uniform.

Lingxu
father

Emily
mother

Shaowei

Family life

Shaowei is an only child, which is very common in China. He lives with his parents, Emily, a publisher, and Lingxu, an engineer. During the week a babysitter takes Shaowei to school and prepares his meals.

Apartment home

Like most people in Beijing, Shaowei and his parents live in an apartment. With so many people living in the city, very few have their own yards.

Remote-controlled robot

Shaowei loves technology. He has a robot, which he can guide around the apartment with a remote control. When he is older, Shaowei would like a job inventing new robots.

"I want to create a robot that can solve everyone's problems."

Yo-yo master

Shaowei enjoys a variety of sports, including table tennis and rock climbing, but his favorite pastime is yo-yoing. He is captain of his class's yo-yo team, and he sometimes enters yo-yo contests.

Shaowei can perform many yo-yo tricks.

Shaowei's school

Shaowei goes to the local elementary school. In addition to regular classes, he has a clarinet lesson once a week. After school, he attends an English class.

Chinese food

Shaowei's favorite food is ice cream, but his family mainly eats Chinese food. Dishes they enjoy include savory buns, *choi sum*, which is similar to spinach, and steamed bread dough.

Choi sum

Savory buns

Steamed bread dough

How I say hello

Ni hao
Pronounced "nee-how"

Where I live

Beijing is in northern China.

Beijing

The Forbidden City is in the center of Beijing. It once housed a royal palace, which is now a museum.

Chinese New Year

Chinese people celebrate their New Year with feasts and fireworks. Shaowei likes this time of year because adults give children money in special red envelopes.

Red envelopes with gifts of money inside are called "red tips."

Growing vegetables

Although Shaowei's family does not have a yard next to their home, they rent a small plot of land nearby. In spring and summer, they grow plenty of vegetables for the family to eat.

Robert

Nine-year-old Robert is from Mongolia, which is between Russia and China. He has many hobbies, including kickboxing, playing soccer and basketball, and making clay models. On special occasions, such as Mongolian New Year, Robert wears a traditional costume made by his grandmother.

Silk scarves are swapped as gifts at Mongolian New Year, which is called *Tsagaan sar*.

Family home
Robert and his family live in Ulaanbaatar, which is the capital of Mongolia. Like many people in the city, Robert lives in an apartment building. The city is a bustling and busy place to live.

Signature

How I say hello
Сайн уу
Pronounced "sain-uu"

Where I live

More than one-third of Mongolia's population live in Ulaanbaatar.

World-famous warrior
This portrait on a hill is of Genghis Khan, a Mongol warlord who built a powerful empire 800 years ago.

Batmunkh
father

Robert

Tara
sister

Antares
brother

Solongo
mother

"My favorite seasons are fall and winter. I like having snowball fights!"

Robert's family
Robert lives with his parents and younger brother and sister. His father was born in the Gobi Desert, in southern Mongolia. His mother is from a part of the country with many mountains.

Fun with clay
Robert enjoys making colorful clay models in the shape of mythical creatures, such as dragons.

The *morin khuur* is also called a horsehead fiddle.

Making music

Robert's father plays a traditional stringed instrument called a *morin khuur*. He often plays it to Robert and his siblings at bedtime.

Boiled meat

Khuushuur

Mongolian food

Robert's family often eats *khuushuur*, which are dumplings filled with ground meat or potato. Boiled meat is also popular, although Robert's favorite foods are pizza and chicken.

Kickboxing kid

Robert has been kickboxing since his father bought him some boxing gloves when he was four years old. He also enjoys playing soccer and basketball.

Riding in the steppe

Robert and his family love exploring their country and plan to visit all of its regions. The steppe, a vast area of grassland, is great for horseback riding.

Living in a yurt

Robert's grandparents live in a yurt in the Gobi Desert. A yurt is a large, round tent that can be quickly put up and taken down again. His grandparents move around the desert with their animals, including camels and horses.

The chimney releases smoke from a stove inside the yurt.

Utako
mother

Sotaro

Taisuke
father

Momo
sister

Sotaro

Sotaro is 10 years old and from Japan in East Asia. He lives on Honshu, the biggest of the many islands that make up Japan. Sotaro has many interests, including swimming and natural history. On special occasions and when practicing martial arts, such as kendo, Sotaro and his sister wear traditional Japanese outfits.

Sotaro wears a *dougi* when he does kendo.

Meet the family

Sotaro lives with his parents, Utako and Taisuke, and his older sister, Momo. His grandmother, Sachiko, lives next door. The family is Buddhist, and they pray to their ancestors every day at the family shrine.

Signature

How I say hello

Konnichiwa
Pronounced "kon-nee-chee-wa"

Where I live

Chiba Prefecture is on the outskirts of Japan's capital city, Tokyo.

Tokyo
More than 38 million people, including Sotaro and his family, live in Tokyo and its outskirts.

Sotaro's house

The family lives in a modern three-story house in Kashiwa, a city in an area known as Chiba Prefecture.

Special writing

Sotaro's grandmother is teaching him *shodo*, which is an ancient style of writing. Instead of a pen or pencil, Sotaro uses a paintbrush dipped in ink to create the intricate Japanese words.

Sotaro's work

Shodo lesson

Avid swimmer

Sotaro is very serious about swimming. He is a member of a swimming team and trains for one-and-a-half hours each day, six days a week! He enters many swimming competitions each year. In winter, Sotaro also skis.

Nishime is simmered root vegetables.

Tofu is made from soybean paste.

Tempura is battered and fried seafood and vegetables.

Fins help Sotaro speed through the water.

Momo wears a patterned kimono when taking part in traditional ceremonies.

Cooked rice is served with most meals.

Miso soup contains seaweed.

Traditional food

Sotaro's family often eats traditional Japanese meals. These are made up of a number of small dishes, almost always including rice and miso soup. There may also be tempura, *nishime*, and tofu. Japanese people eat with chopsticks, rather than knives and forks.

"Every day I try to catch insects and other animals. I also try to catch fish from the rivers."

Science books

Science and nature

At school, Sotaro's favorite subject is science, and he wants to be a biologist when he is older. He visits his local nature preserve as often as possible and looks out for animals, such as beetles and turtles. Sotaro also keeps some animals, including a nonpoisonous snake, as pets.

Pet snake

Sotaro and Momo in the nature preserve

Yeh-Lin

Yeh-Lin lives in Seoul, the capital city of South Korea, in East Asia. Seoul is home to about one-fifth of South Korea's population and is the world's most "wired" city, with most homes having high-speed internet access. Yeh-Lin loves living in Seoul because her home is near her favorite amusement park.

SeungHyun
mother

Chae-Lin
sister

Sae-Lin
sister

Teenie

Yeh-Lin

My family

Yeh-Lin is nine years old and has two sisters—Chae-Lin, who is 12 years old, and Sae-Lin, who is seven years old. They live with their mother, SeungHyun, and pet dog, Teenie.

Bobblehead

One of Yeh-Lin's favorite toys is a cuddly Winnie the Pooh pillow. He is the main character from a series of well-known children's books.

Yeh-Lin's school uniform

Music makers

Yeh-Lin and her sisters are all talented musicians. Yeh-Lin plays the clarinet, Chae-Lin plays the flute, and Sae-Lin plays the violin. The girls practice at home and often perform at school.

High-rise home

About 70 percent of South Korea is covered in mountains, so most of the population lives in towns and cities. To save space, most people, including Yeh-Lin, live in apartments in high-rise buildings.

School days

Yeh-Lin enjoys school so much that she wants to be a teacher when she's older. However, there's one thing that Yeh-Lin does not like about school—exams. When she's a teacher, she will never make her class take tests!

Elementary school

Yeh-Lin attends a large elementary school near her home. In South Korea, children start school at the age of eight.

Yeh-Lin's painting shows a traditional Korean mask and drum.

Schoolbook

Yeh-Lin's schoolbook contains fun cartoons to help her learn math.

After-school clubs

Yeh-Lin attends after-school clubs, where she practices things such as art, reading, and science. She enjoys using her imagination and painting colorful pictures.

Signature

박 예린

How I say hello

Anyong haseyo
Pronounced "an-yong ha-SAY-yo"

Where I live

Seoul is located on the Han River, in the northwest of the country.

Seoul

Seoul is so huge that it is divided into 25 separate districts, called *gu*. Yeh-Lin lives in Gangdong-gu.

South Korean food

Most people in South Korea eat rice every day. Yeh-Lin's family has rice with savory meals and also makes it into sweet treats called *songpyeon*.

Seaweed broth

Rice

Bulgogi (marinated beef)

Dried seaweed

Dinner tray

Kimchi (chili pickled cabbage)

Spicy stir-fried dried squid

Sweet rice cakes

Songpyeon

National dress

On special occasions, such as Korean Thanksgiving (*Chuseok*) or New Year, Yeh-Lin wears a traditional dress called a *hanbok*. The dress reaches the floor and has a full skirt. It is often brightly colored.

Anju
mother

Jagtar
father

Mehak

Manvi
sister

Mehak

Mehak is eight years old. She lives with her family in New Delhi, the capital city of India. Mehak wears traditional Indian clothes on special occasions, such as the Hindu festival Diwali, a festival of lights. Mehak mostly speaks Hindi, but like many Indians she can also speak and write in English.

This item of clothing is called a sari.

Meet the family
Mehak lives with her family in an apartment building near the center of the city. Her father works as a book designer, while her mother looks after the home and the children.

Mehak's apartment

"I have to work hard at school, because I want to be a doctor."

Spicy food
Lots of Indian food is very spicy. *Thali* is a typical north Indian meal that consists of several small dishes. It usually includes *dhal*, rice, vegetable curry, and bread.

Roti is a popular Indian flat bread.

Dhal is a dish of spiced lentils.

Fun with dyes
Hindus celebrate many festivals, including Holi. In the spring, Mehak enjoys the Holi ritual of throwing colorful dyes over everyone.

New Delhi
Mehak lives in one of the busiest cities in India. It is home to lots of amazing architecture.

How I say hello

Khammaghani
Pronounced "khome-ma-gunny"

Where I live

Vishnu lives near the Thar Desert. On the other side of the desert lies Pakistan.

Bishnoi temple
Once a year, Vishnu's family visits the Bishnoi temple near Khejarli, about 6 miles (10 km) from home.

Vishnu

Ten-year-old Vishnu lives in the state of Rajasthan, in western India. Vishnu and his family are Bishnoi, which means they live their lives by 29 sacred principles laid down by a spiritual leader called Guru Jambheshwar. The Bishnoi care deeply for animals and the environment.

Pet calf
Vishnu has a pet calf, whom he is very fond of. He loves to take care of trees and animals, in particular black bucks, a type of antelope that roams near his home.

Aenchi
grandmother

Oma
father

Mahendar
brother

Goredaen
grandfather

Parsi
mother

Mamta
sister

Vishnu

Nirmal
sister

Cricket fan
The most popular sport in India is cricket, and it's one of Vishnu's favorite hobbies. In the game, teams take turns trying to get the most runs by hitting a ball with a wooden bat.

Home life
Vishnu lives with his parents, siblings, and grandparents. The family lives in huts with thatched roofs. These buildings are perfect for staying cool in the heat.

Murk

Murk is seven years old and lives in Pakistan. Like 97 percent of the population of Pakistan, Murk is a Muslim. Her favorite time of year is Eid, which is when Muslims celebrate with friends and family after fasting (limiting when they eat) for a month. Aside from Eid, Murk's favorite thing is her pet goat.

Murk's pet goat

Murk wears a traditional *salwar kameez* (pants and tunic) with a scarf covering her hair.

Hameeda
mother

Maira
sister

Abdul
father

Wazeera
grandmother

Tahir
brother

Allah Wasayo
grandfather

Tahira
sister

Tarique
brother

Maqbool
brother

Murk

Big family

Murk lives with her parents, grandparents, and younger brothers and sisters. Lots of other members of her family live nearby, and Murk loves it when they come to visit.

Cooking area

Murk's mother, Hameeda, prepares all the food for the family, although Murk sometimes helps. Hameeda cooks the food in big metal pots over a fire in an outbuilding.

Murk's classroom

Murk celebrates Independence Day at school with flags and banners.

Murk uses a fingerprint to make her signature.

How I say hello

Salaamu
Pronounced "sa-laa-moo"

Where I live

Murk lives in the Sindh region in southeast Pakistan.

Murk's education

Murk loves school and would like to become a teacher one day. In addition to going to regular school, she attends a special religious school called a *madrasa* twice a day to learn all about Islam.

Textbook

Backyard
Murk spends a lot of time in her backyard because it's where her pet goat lives.

Moong dal

Favorite food

Murk's favorite meal is a lentil dish called *moong dal*, which is usually served with rice. Lentils are seeds that are very rich in protein. Other local specialties include chicken *karahi*, a type of curry, and *saag*, or spinach curry.

Chicken karahi

Saag

Celebrating Pakistan's Independence Day

Clay pots

Murk's name means "smile," and nothing makes her smile more than making clay pots. Once they have dried in the sunshine, she paints them different colors.

Hand art

On special occasions, female Muslims decorate their hands using dye from a plant called henna. Murk has her hands decorated to celebrate Eid—she thinks it looks beautiful.

"I love the Muslim festival Eid. We wear special clothes and gather with friends and relatives."

Bolat

Bolat is eight years old and lives in Astana, the capital city of Kazakhstan, in Central Asia. In his spare time, Bolat likes to play the *dombra*, a long-necked, stringed instrument. He also likes rollerblading, cycling, and playing with his pet dog. Bolat wears special clothes for *Nauryz*, or Kazakh New Year, which is a very important festival in Kazakhstan.

Islyambek grandfather

Roza mother

Yerbol father

Baglan grandmother

Aruzhan sister

Bolat

Asylzhan sister

... Bolat wears traditional Kazakh clothes on special occasions and festivals.

Bolat's family

Bolat's father, Yerbol, is in the army and his mother, Roza, works as a kindergarten teacher. In Kazakhstan, it is a custom for the oldest child to be brought up by the grandparents, so Bolat is very close to his grandmother and grandfather.

Family house

Bolat's parents, twin sisters, and grandparents all live together in the same house in a district of Astana. Bolat likes living in the city because it is a busy place, full of many exciting things to see and do.

The *dombra* has two strings.

Playtime

Bolat enjoys playing outside, especially rollerblading and cycling. He also likes to play the board game checkers with his father.

Kazakhstan is in Asia but is also close to Europe.

Teatime

Food and drink

Bolat's family makes tea using a kettle that is kept in the yard. Bolat's favorite food is *beshbarmak*, a traditional Kazakh meal made of horse meat and pasta.

Horse cheese

Kaymak is a thick cream.

Shelpek is flat, fried dough.

Beshbarmak

Baursak is fried dough balls.

Sary mai is butter.

Bayterek Tower
From the top of this monument, you can see all across Astana.

Bolat's schoolbooks

"When I'm at home, I like to spend time playing with my dog."

Star pupil

Bolat is a dedicated student. At the end of the school year, he was presented with a certificate and sash for doing so well.

Pet dogs

Bolat's family has two dogs, but his favorite is Bobik. Bolat helps to look after the dogs by feeding them each day.

Bolat's school

Shalom
Pronounced "sha-LOM"

Where I live

Erel lives about 35 miles (60 km) from each of Israel's two main cities, Tel Aviv and Jerusalem.

Jerusalem
The city of Jerusalem is an incredibly important place for the Jewish, Christian, and Muslim religions.

Erel

Seven-year-old Erel is from Israel, a country in the Middle East. The northern part of Israel is mountainous with cold winters, but the southern part has a hot desert climate. Erel lives in the warmer south, close to the beach. Her hobbies include playing soccer and trampolining. She also likes to play the piano.

Summer fun

In summer, Erel enjoys visiting the beach. She likes to explore the sand dunes and play a bat-and-ball game called *matkot*.

Pomegranate seeds

Fish head

Green peas

Apples with honey

Orit mother

Sagi father

Shalev brother

Erel

Yahav brother

New Year

Erel is Jewish. Her family is not religious, but they celebrate all the Jewish holidays. At Jewish New Year, different foods have special meanings. Apples with honey, for example, are believed to bring a sweet new year.

Family home

Erel lives in a village called a *moshav*. This is a very close-knit community where everyone helps one another. She lives with her parents, her brothers, and their pet cat.

Erel's house

"I want to clean up the oceans, so the turtles and other ocean animals won't die from all the garbage in the water."

Khalifa

Khalifa is six years old and from Bahrain, an Arab country in the Middle East. Bahrain is made up of more than 80 islands and is more than 90 percent hot desert. Khalifa likes soccer, drawing, and gardening. He is a Muslim and wears a long tunic called a *thobe* for special occasions such as the festival of Eid.

This patterned scarf is called a *keffiyeh*.

Family home

Family life

Khalifa lives with his parents and his two younger brothers, three-year-old Saif and baby Mishal. The family loves soccer and supports Tottenham Hotspur, from the English Premier League.

Omar father

Mishal brother

Sarah mother

Khalifa

Saif brother

Signature

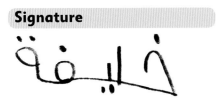

How I say hello

Salam alaykum
Pronounced "sa-LAM al-aye-CUM"

Where I live

Khalifa lives in Manama, Bahrain's capital city.

Modern city

Manama is the largest city in Bahrain and about one-eighth of its population lives there.

Gardening

Khalifa's family has a housekeeper, Helen, who cooks most of their food. She also grows vegetables for the family and is teaching Khalifa how to garden.

Pet parrot

Khalifa's father, Omar, has a "talking" African gray parrot named Johana. Khalifa and his brothers, however, have nicknamed her Bubs.

Southeast Asia and Australasia

Pho
A classic Vietnamese dish, *pho* combines noodles, chicken or beef, and vegetables in a broth.

Southeast Asia isn't actually a continent, but a region within Asia. It is a hot and humid part of the world, with thousands of beautiful beaches. To the south, it joins up with Australasia, a vast area that includes the largest island in the world, Australia, as well as thousands of smaller islands that dot the surface of the Pacific Ocean.

FACT FILE

Population
625 million in Southeast Asia
40 million in Australasia

Number of countries
11 in Southeast Asia
14 in Australasia

Biggest city by population
More than 10 million people live in Jakarta, the capital of Indonesia.

Longest river

The Mekong River flows through five Southeast Asian countries and China.

Highest mountain
Hkakabo Razi in Myanmar is believed to be the region's highest peak, but its exact height is unknown.

Temples of Angkor
Parts of this 10th to 13th-century temple complex in northern Cambodia have been completely taken over by the jungle.

Kangaroo
Australia is home to animals not seen anywhere else on Earth. Kangaroos are large mammals that get around by hopping.

The Great Barrier Reef
Lying off the coast of northeast Australia, this huge coral reef is home to thousands of species, including the hawksbill turtle.

Aboriginal festival
Every year a festival is held in the state of Queensland, Australia, to celebrate the culture of the native Aboriginal people.

Thailand
Find Knight on page 70

Philippines

Vietnam
Find Tai on pages 72–73

Papua New Guinea

Samoa

Solomon Islands

Myanmar
(Burma)

Laos

Vietnam

Thailand

Cambodia

Philippines

Palau

Brunei

Malaysia

Singapore

Indonesia

East
Timor

Micronesia

Marshall
Islands

Nauru

Papua New
Guinea

Solomon Islands

Kiribati

Tuvalu

Samoa

Fiji

Vanuatu

Tonga

Australia

New Zealand

Fiji

Malaysia
Find Ivan on page 71

Indonesia

East Timor

Australia
Find Clara and Lucy on page 75

Australia
Find Andre on page 74

New Zealand
Find Jamie on pages 76–77

Knight

Naiyarat, better known as Knight, is eight years old. He is from Thailand in Southeast Asia. About 95 percent of Thai people follow the Buddhist religion, including Knight and his family. Knight's wide range of interests include piano playing, drawing, and high-kicking taekwondo!

"My favorite time of year is summer, because I get 75 days off school!"

Nualrat
aunt

Akarat
father

Waleerat
mother

Rattanapon
grandmother

Knight

Home life

Knight lives with his parents, who are teachers, his aunt, Nualrat, and grandma, Rattanapon. Knight likes spending time with his family—he exercises with his grandma every day!

Knight's house

... Knight wears a white taekwondo uniform called a *dobok*.

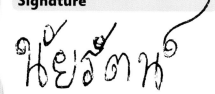
How I say hello

Sawadee
Pronounced "Sa-wa-dee"

Where I live

Thailand is situated between the Indian Ocean and the South China Sea.

Creative fun

In addition to playing the piano and singing, budding artist Knight loves to paint and draw. He paints with his mother often and has won his school's art competition twice!

A bowl of *tom yum kung* soup ....

Thai food

Knight's grandma cooks traditional Thai dishes for the family, such as *tom yum kung*, a popular spicy shrimp soup. Knight's favorite foods are salmon and steak.

Bangkok
Knight is from Bangkok, the capital of Thailand. More than 8 million people live there.

Ivan

Seven-year-old Ivan lives in Malaysia, in Southeast Asia. Ivan and his family follow an ancient Chinese tradition of religion and philosophy called Taoism. They also celebrate Chinese New Year, which takes place in January or February. Each Chinese year is named after an animal, such as a dragon or snake.

Ivan's home in Klang

Meet the family

Ivan lives with his parents, older brother, Jensen, younger sister, Amanda, and his grandparents. Both Ivan's parents are sales executives and Ivan thinks he'd like to become one, too, when he finishes school.

Steven father

Jasmine mother

Ang grandmother

Amanda sister

Ivan

Jensen brother

Traditional cakes decorated to look like tortoise shells

Malaysian treats

Ivan loves sweets! Malaysian candies and cakes are brightly colored and made with ingredients like palm sugar, rice flour, and coconut.

How I say hello

Apa khabar
Pronounced "Apa ka-bar"

Where I live

Ivan lives in Klang, near the capital of Malaysia, Kuala Lumpur.

Record breaker

Kuala Lumpur's Petronas Towers were the world's tallest buildings from 1998–2004.

"My hero is the martial artist Bruce Lee, because he beats all the bad guys."

Taoism

Ivan's family has a table of worship in their house. They worship many different gods as part of their Taoist beliefs. Taoism encourages goodness and harmony with nature.

Signature

How I say hello

Xin chào
Pronounced "sin chow"

Where I live

Vietnam is in Southeast Asia. The Mekong River enters the sea at the Vietnamese coast. This creates the delta where Tai lives.

......Tai's houseboat

Tai

Tai is eight years old and lives in Vietnam in Southeast Asia. Tai lives with his parents and sister on a houseboat on the Mekong Delta. Tai's favorite time of year is the Vietnamese New Year, or *Tet* festival. During this time, it is tradition for everyone to stop working and for families to come together and celebrate.

"I want to be a police officer when I grow up, so that I can help my community and fight crime."

Han
sister

Kim-Chuong
mother

Luom
father

Tai

Tai's family

Tai lives with his father, Luom, who is a guitarist, his mother, Kim-Chuong, who sells drinks at the floating market, and Han, his 11-year-old sister. Tai and his family are practicing Buddhists.

Tai's family sells durians—a strong-smelling fruit that only grows in Southeast Asia. ......

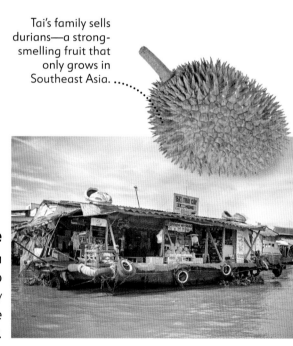

Riverboat home

The family's houseboat doubles as a café, and they sell fruit and drinks to passers-by. In high season, the family can make up to 500,000 Vietnamese dong ($22) per day.

When it is too hot, Tai likes to jump into the river to cool down.

Having fun

Tai loves to play in the water and swims to other boats in the area to visit his friends. Tai likes to play, but his studies and chores are also very important. He often helps out on the boat by serving drinks or selling fruit.

Vietnam is a warm country so Tai often wears a T-shirt and shorts to keep cool.

Getting around

Tai travels to and from school by boat. However, when traveling on land the family uses a scooter. Tai's sister, Han, cycles to school every day, which takes her about 10 minutes. One day, Tai would like his own bicycle so that he doesn't have to go to school by boat.

Sweet and salty fish

Tai likes to play with water pistols with his friends. Big guns are best because they can hold lots of water!

Ca kho tau

Bean sprouts

Dinnertime

One traditional Vietnamese dish is *canh ca chua*, a sour soup made with Mekong river fish, pineapple, tomatoes, and bean sprouts. Tai's favorite food is stir-fried chicken with fish sauce and garlic.

Mekong river fish

Canh ca chua ingredients

Tomato

Local schools

Tai and Han go to different schools. They both have an early start and finish their classes at 10:30 in the morning. This gives them plenty of time to do their homework and to help out on the boat. Tai's favorite subject at school is math.

Tai usually likes to go barefoot when he's on the boat.

73

Andre

Eleven-year-old Andre lives in Melbourne, Australia. Andre is a proud descendant of Australia's Aboriginal people, whose culture stretches back more than 60,000 years. Like many Australian kids, Andre is an enthusiastic Aussie Rules football player and one day hopes to play professionally.

Home in the trees

Andre lives with his grandparents, Karen and Rodrick, in the Yarra Valley. Their house is surrounded by tall gum trees and ferns.

Andre's home

Karen grandmother **Rodrick** grandfather

Aussie Rules football is played with an oval-shaped ball.

Signature

How I say hello

Hello
Pronounced "he-LO"

Where I live

Andre lives near the city of Melbourne, in southeastern Australia.

Healesville Sanctuary

Andre enjoys visiting the local animal sanctuary and hanging out with native animals, such as koalas.

Witchetty grubs

Bush tucker

Australian Aboriginals sometimes eat food caught in the Australian countryside, or "bush." This is called "bush tucker" and includes witchetty grubs and kangaroos.

Aboriginal traditions

Andre learns a lot about his culture from his grandparents. He has learned how to play the didgeridoo, a traditional Aboriginal instrument.

Andre playing the didgeridoo

Boomerang

Clara and Lucy

Clara and Lucy are twins from Australia. They are both nine years old, but Lucy is two minutes older than Clara! Both sisters love animals. Clara wants to be a vet when she grows up, while Lucy wants to be a horseback rider. They have a pet dog, named Holly, who was a rescue puppy.

"When I grow up, I want to live on a ranch with my sister, Lucy."

Home life

The twins live with their parents and 12-year-old brother, Riley, in Blackburn, a peaceful suburb of the city of Melbourne.

Lisa
mother

Rupert
father

Lucy   Holly   Clara   Riley
brother

Family home

Signatures

Clara   Lucy

How I say hello

G'day
Pronounced "guh-day"

Where I live

Melbourne is in the Australian state of Victoria.

Feeding the ducks

The sisters live near a beautiful lake where they go for walks and visit the ducks.

School uniform

Like all Australian children, Clara and Lucy have to wear hats to school every day. This is to protect their heads from the sun when they play outside.

Pavlova

In the summer, the family eats pavlova, a tasty dessert made of fresh fruit, meringue, and whipped cream.

Holly is a cocker spaniel.

Gymnastics stars

Both Clara and Lucy are members of a gymnastics team and practice twice a week. They recently received trophies for coming third in a big competition!

Jamie

Eight-year-old Jamie is from New Zealand. He is a big rugby fan and is very proud of his national team, the All Blacks. Despite being home to only 4.6 million people, New Zealand has one of the best rugby teams in the world. Here, Jamie is doing the haka, the traditional Maori war dance, which the All Blacks perform before every match.

Jamie wears his All Blacks uniform whenever he can.

Taunaha
mother

Wayne
father

Ethan
brother

Jamie   **Alexander**   **Braeden**
brother   brother

Family

Jamie lives with his parents and three brothers. Jamie's mother, Taunaha, is a Maori. The Maoris were the first people to arrive in New Zealand, in the 13th century, long before Europeans settled there in the 19th century. Maori culture is very important in New Zealand.

Coastal home

Jamie's house is very close to the sea. This means that when Jamie and his brothers get bored with playing in their backyard, they just head to the beach, where Jamie likes to go swimming.

Jamie's rugby ball was signed by the All Blacks.

Sea urchin

Urchin roe

Beach food

The beach isn't just a place to play. Jamie and his brothers like to search the rock pools for sea urchins—called *kina* in Maori—to eat. Their mother is an expert at removing the spiky shells to find the tasty eggs, called roe, inside.

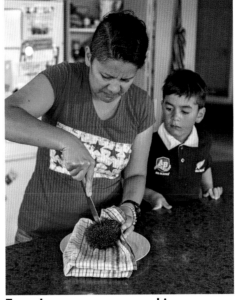
Taunaha opens up a sea urchin.

How I say hello

Kia ora
Pronounced "kee or-uh"

Where I live

New Zealand is in the southwestern Pacific Ocean.

Bay of Islands
Jamie lives in the Bay of Islands in the far north of New Zealand's North Island.

Maori culture

Maori culture is a big part of Jamie's family life. On special occasions, his grandfather cooks a traditional *hangi* meal, using hot stones placed in a pit oven dug in the ground then covered in dirt. Jamie also likes to visit the nearby Waitangi Treaty Grounds to see the special Maori canoes, called *waka taua*, that are housed there.

> "I belong to the United Kawakawa Under 8s rugby team. When I grow up, I want to be an All Black."

Special beads

When he was younger, Jamie had a form of cancer called leukemia and was very sick for three years. Every time he faced a treatment or challenge, he received a bead. Now the beads remind Jamie how happy he is to be strong and healthy.

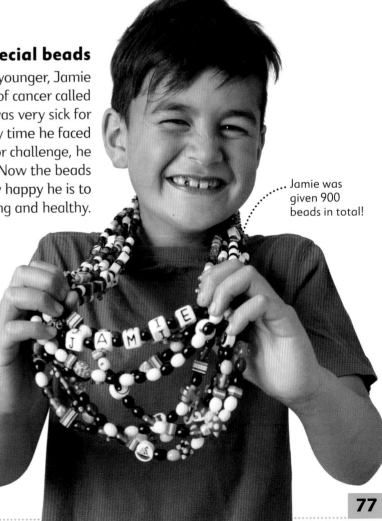

Jamie was given 900 beads in total!

Home brew

Jamie drinks *kombucha*, a special tea, to stay healthy. His mother makes it by adding yeast and bacteria to sweetened tea and leaving it to brew for at least a week. It tastes better than it sounds!

Glossary

animal sanctuary Place where tame or wild animals are brought to live and are protected. The animals usually spend the rest of their lives in the sanctuary, although some may later be released into the wild

apartment Home that is part of a larger, often high-rise, building.

architect Someone who designs, or makes the plans for, buildings and other structures

Australian rules football Ball game played between two teams, each with 18 players. The aim is to score goals by kicking an oval-shaped ball through goal posts. Also called Aussie rules

Bishnoi Someone who follows a religion called Bishnoism, which was founded in India and has a great respect for wildlife, trees, and the environment

Buddhist Member of a religion called Buddhism, which follows the teachings of the Buddha, who lived in India about 2,500 years ago

bunting Colorful decorations such as small flags and ribbons for a festive occasion

capital city City in a country or region where decisions are made by leaders that affect how the rest of the country or region is run

carnival Special event in which people dress up and parade through the streets with music and dancing. The Rio Carnival in Brazil is the world's biggest carnival

Catholic Someone who follows a type of Christianity called Catholicism. The head of the Catholic Church is called the Pope and lives in Vatican City in Rome

cheerleaders People who dance and shout out songs or chant to entertain the supporters at sports events, such as football and basketball games

Cheerleaders

Christian Someone who follows the teachings of Jesus Christ, who lived in the Middle East 2,000 years ago

Christmas Christian festival marking the birth of Jesus Christ on December 25

clarinet Musical instrument in the woodwind family, which is played by blowing air through it

continent One of seven very large areas of land, such as Europe and North America, that make up the world

cricket Ball game played between two teams of 11 players. The goal is to score runs by hitting a hard round ball, bowled by a member of the opposing team, and running between two sets of wooden markers called wickets

delta Area of flat land near the coast where a river breaks up into many smaller rivers before entering the sea

district Area of a town, city, or country

Eid Muslim festival, often referring to the celebration at the end of Ramadan, which is the month of fasting

engineer Someone who uses science and math to solve technical problems

festival Celebration or special event, often with music and dancing

First Communion Christian ceremony that welcomes a person into the Christian Church

haka War dance with chanting, traditionally performed by New Zealand's Maori warriors before a battle, or by New Zealand rugby players before a match

Halloween October 31, when some children dress up and go trick-or-treating, in which they knock on neighbors' doors asking for candy

Hindu Member of the Indian religion Hinduism. Hindus worship many gods and believe that when people die they are born again

houseboat Boat used as a home

Kimono

Jew Follower of the religion Judaism. Jews worship one god and their holy books are the Old Testament and the Talmud

kimono Traditional Japanese long robe

LEGO Colorful, interlocking, plastic, toy building bricks

monkey bars Piece of playground equipment with an overhead horizontal ladder that children can hang from or swing across

monument Statue, building, or other structure put up to honor or remember an important person or historical event

mosque Place of worship for Muslims

Muslim Someone whose religion is Islam. Muslims believe in one god, and they follow the teachings of Prophet Muhammad

Native American reservation Area of land in North America looked after, or managed, by one or more Native American tribes

outskirts Outer areas of a town or city

population Number of people living in a region, such as a town, city, or country

robot Machine that can be instructed, or programmed, to do a complicated task or a series of movements

rugby Ball game played between two teams, each with 13 or 15 players. The goal is to score points by getting an oval-shaped ball to the end line of the opposing team's half of the field

scouting Worldwide organization for children that teaches useful skills, such as how to survive outdoors

soccer Ball game played between two teams of 11 players. The goal is to score goals by kicking a round ball into the opposing team's net.

sibling Brother or sister

signature Your way of writing your name

s'more North American treat made up of a roasted marshmallow and a slab of chocolate sandwiched between two pieces of graham cracker. Short for "something more."

S'more

specialty Food or dish that a particular region is famous for making

Taoist Someone who follows an ancient Chinese religion called Taoism, which has many gods

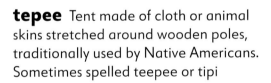

Tepee

tepee Tent made of cloth or animal skins stretched around wooden poles, traditionally used by Native Americans. Sometimes spelled teepee or tipi

traditional Word that describes something that people have done for a long time. For example, traditional clothes are a style of clothing that people have worn for a long time, often hundreds of years

trampolining Jumping or tumbling on a trampoline, which is a tough sheet of cloth attached by springs to a sturdy frame

tributary Stream or river that flows into a bigger river

veld Large area of flat land covered in grass or bushes, found in southern African countries. Also spelled veldt

X-ray Special image that shows your bones and the inside of your body

yurt Large, round tent used as a home by people who move from place to place in some countries, including Mongolia

Index

A

Aboriginals, Australian 68, 74
Aconcagua (Argentina) 16
Addis Ababa (Ethiopia) 41
Africa 38–49
Amazon River 16
Andes 16
Angel Falls (Venezuela) 16
Angkor, Temples of (Cambodia) 68
Argentina 16–17, 20–21
art 10, 15, 59, 70
Asia 50–73
Astana (Kazakhstan) 64
Athens (Greece) 32
Aussie Rules 74
Australasia 70–71, 74–77
Australia 69, 74–75

B

Bahrain 51, 67
Bangkok (Thailand) 70
Barcelona (Spain) 33
baseball 6, 13
Bay of Islands (New Zealand) 77
Bayterek Tower (Astana) 65
Beijing (China) 52–53
Berbers 40
Bishnoi 61
Botswana 39, 44–45
Brazil 16–17, 18–19
Buddhists 50, 56, 70, 72
Buenos Aires (Argentina) 20–21

C

Canada 6–7, 8
Carnival (Rio) 19
Catholics 21
Charlotte (South Carolina, USA) 10
cheerleaders 10
China 50–51, 52–53
Christians 9, 12, 21, 41, 44, 48
Christmas 21, 34
climbing 36, 52
Colombia 16–17, 22–23

Colosseum (Rome) 24
cricket 61
cycling 29, 31, 64, 73

D E F

Denali (Alaska) 6
Día de Muertos (Day of the Dead) 15
Eid 62, 63, 67
Elbruss, Mount (Russia) 24
England 26
Ethiopia 39, 41
Europe 24–37
Everest, Mount 50
farms 9, 27, 42–43, 47
Finland 25, 28
fjords (Norway) 24
football 10
France 25, 30–31

G

Gaelic football 27
gardening 32, 35, 53, 67
Gdańsk (Poland) 29
Genghis Khan 54
Germany 25, 34–35
Ghana 39, 46
Gobi Desert 54, 55
golf 20
Grand Canyon (Arizona, USA) 6
Great Barrier Reef (Australia) 68
Great Wall of China 50
Greece 25, 32
Greeks, Ancient 24, 32
gymnastics 9, 10, 75

H I J

Halloween 9, 12
Helsinki (Finland) 28
henna 63
Hindus 60
Hkakabo Razi (Myanmar) 68
Holi 60
horseback riding 35, 55
Huixquilucan (Mexico) 15
ice hockey 28

Incas 16
India 51, 60–61
Ireland 25, 27
Israel 51, 66
Jakarta (Indonesia) 68
Japan 50–51, 56–57
Jerusalem (Israel) 66
jewelry 43, 45, 77
Jews 66
Jordan 66–67
judo 31
jumping rope 41, 48

K L

Kalahari Desert 44
Kazakhstan 51, 64–65
kendo 56
kickboxing 55
Kilimanjaro, Mount (Tanzania) 38
Kuala Lumpur (Malaysia) 71
Lagos (Nigeria) 38
Lego 26, 31, 37
leukemia 77
Lyon (France) 31

M

Maasai people 42–43
Machu Picchu (Peru) 16
madrasas 63
Malaysia 69, 71
Manama (Bahrain) 67
Mandela, Nelson 47
Maoris 76–77
Marrakech (Morocco) 40
matkot 66
Mayan people 6
Mekong Delta (Vietnam) 72
Mekong River 68
Melbourne (Australia) 74, 75
Mexico 6–7, 14–15
Mexico City 6, 15
Middle East 66–67
Mississippi-Missouri-Jefferson River (USA) 6
Mongolia 51, 54–55
Montana (USA) 12–13

Monteria (Colombia) 22
Montreal (Canada) 8
Morocco 39, 40
Moscow (Russia) 24, 37
moshav 66
Muslims 40, 47, 62–63, 67

N

Nancy (France) 30
Native Americans 12–13
Nelspruit (South Africa) 49
New Delhi (India) 60
New Jersey (USA) 11
New Year
  Chinese 53, 71
  Jewish 66
  Nauryz (Kazakhstan) 64
  Tet (Vietnam) 72
  Tsagaan sar (Mongolia) 54
New York City (USA) 11
New Zealand 69, 76–77
Nile River 38
North America 6–15

O P

Ohio (USA) 9
oware 46
Pakistan 51, 62–63
Petronas Towers (Kuala Lumpur) 71
Poland 25, 26, 29
Pretoria (South Africa) 47
pyramids (Egypt) 38

R

rain forests 16, 38
Rajasthan (India) 61
reservations, Native American 12
Reyes Magos (Three Wise Men) 21
Rio de Janeiro (Brazil) 18
riverboats 72
robots 37, 52
rollerblading 64, 65
Romans 24, 31
Ruaha National Park (Tanzania) 42

rugby 76, 77
Russia 24–25, 37

S

sailing 36
Sakumono Township (Ghana) 46
San tribe 44–45
São Paolo (Brazil) 16
scouts 14
Seoul (South Korea) 58–59
Shawnee tribe 12
shodo writing 56
skateboarding 18, 19
skiing 29, 36, 57
soccer 18, 20, 22, 33, 41, 66, 67
South Africa 39, 47–49
South America 16–23
South Carolina (USA) 10
South Korea 51, 58–59
Southeast Asia 68–73
Spain 25, 33
spina bifida 48–49
Stockholm (Sweden) 36
street dance 28
Sweden 36

T

taekwondo 70
Tanzania 38, 39, 42–43
Taoism 71
teepees 13
Thailand 69, 70
Tokyo (Japan) 50, 56
trampolining 8, 36, 66
Tsonga people 49

U V W Y

Ulaanbaatar (Mongolia) 54
USA 6–7, 9–13
Vielau (Germany) 34–35
Vietnam 69, 72–73
Volga River 24
Winchester (England) 26
Yangtze River 50
yo-yos 52, 53
yurts 55

Acknowledgments

DORLING KINDERSLEY would like to thank Caroline Hunt for proofreading, Helen Peters for the index, and Simon Mumford for his help with the maps. DK would also like to thank everyone who helped to organize the photoshoots, in particular Latifa Aliza, Martha Hardy, Maham Ali, Noor Jehan Dhanani, Anne and Greg Laws, and Fulbridge Academy. Most importantly, DK would like to say a massive thank you to all of the children and families featured in this book!

The publisher would like to thank the following for their kind permission to reproduce their photographs:

(Key: a-above; b-below/bottom; c-center; f-far; l-left; r-right; t-top)

6 Corbis: Macduff Everton (cla); Radius Images (crb); Robert Michael (b). **Dorling Kindersley:** Greg Ward / Rough Guides (clb). **Getty Images:** Andrew Burton (cr); Independent Picture Service / Universal Images Group (cra). **7 Alamy Images:** Jim Lane (bc). **Corbis:** 68 / Ocean (clb); Michio Hoshino / Minden Pictures (tl); Yew! Images (fclb); David Turnley (fbl). **Getty Images:** Chris Jackson (fbr); Elmer Martinez / AFP (br). **8 Corbis:** Philippe Renault / Hemis (br). **15 Dorling Kindersley:** Sony Computer Entertainment Europe / Sanzaru Games (fcra). **iStockphoto.com:** maogg (fcla, cla). **16 Alamy Images:** AM Corporation / Aflo Co. Ltd. (fcrb); Alice Nerr (fcla); Florian Kopp / imageBROKER (fcr); Kuttig - Travel (bl); FB-Fischer / imageBROKER (fbr). **Dorling Kindersley:** Suzanne Porter / Rough Guides (cr). **naturepl.com:** Bert Willaert (tc). **17 Alamy Images:** Anthony Asael (tl); Danny Manzanares (tr); Heiner Heine / imageBROKER (ftr/girl); Wilmar Photography (ftr); Mercedes Soledad Manrique (fclb); Lafforgue Eric / hemis.fr (clb); Thomas Cockrem (fbr). **Corbis:** Annie Belt (fcr). **Dreamstime.com:** Chicco7 (cl); Sjors737 (crb). **Getty Images:** Domino / Photodisc (br).

18 National Geographic Creative: Mike Theiss (b). **21 Corbis:** Lawton / Photocuisine (clb); Jeremy Woodhouse / Masterfile (b). **Getty Images:** FotografiaBasica / E+ (cb). **22 Alamy Images:** EPA European Pressphoto Agency B.V (cl). **24 Alamy Images:** ITAR-TASS Photo Agency (cr). **Corbis:** Sergei Bobylev / ITAR-TASS Photo Agency (cra); Serguei Fomine / Global Look (crb). **Dorling Kindersley:** Getty Images / Stockbyte / John Foxx (ca). **iStockphoto.com:** Nikolay Tsuguliev / Tsuguliev (cl). **25 Alamy Images:** Bosiljka Zutich (bc). **Getty Images:** Paul Biris / Moment (cra); Ragnar Th. Sigurdsson / age fotostock (fclb); Holger Leue / Lonely Planet Images (fcr); Hilary Helton / Photolibrary (fcrb). **28 Getty Images:** Milamai / Moment Open (fbl). **32 Dorling Kindersley:** Michelle Grant / Rough Guides (fbr). **33 Corbis:** Lucas Vallecillos / ZUMA Press (cra). **37 Getty Images:** Vladimir Zakharov / Moment (bl). **38 Corbis:** Peter Groenendijk / robertharding (b). **Getty Images:** Sean Caffrey / Lonely Planet Images (cr); Tim Laman / National Geographic (cl); Mike D. Kock / Gallo Images (fcr). **39 Corbis:** Anthony Asael / Art in All of Us (tl). **Getty Images:** JD Dollet / arabianEye (cr); Ken Scicluna / AWL Images (tc); John Warburton-Lee / AWL Images (cra); Guy Moberly / Lonely Planet Images (fcl); yoh4nn / E+ (fclb); Nigel Pavitt / AWL Images (bl); Ariadne Van Zandbergen / Lonely Planet Images (bc). **40 Getty Images:** Amaia Arozena & Gotzon Iraola / Moment Open (bl). **41 Getty Images:** Aaron Huey / National Geographic (bl). **49 Getty Images:** Ullstein Bild (cr). **50 Alamy Images:** Sean Pavone (cra). **Corbis:** Spaces Images / Blend

Images (b). **Getty Images:** Demetrio Carrasco / AWL Images (crb); Eric PHAN-KIM / Moment (cr). **51 Getty Images:** Ishara S. Kodikara / AFP (bl); Hans Neleman / The Image Bank (tr); Steven L. Raymer / National Geographic (cla); Jane Sweeney / Lonely Planet Images (cl). **54 Corbis:** Christophe Boisvieux (bl). **56 Getty Images:** Roevin / Moment (fbl). **59 Dorling Kindersley:** Martin Richardson / Rough Guides (cr). **67 Corbis:** Jane Sweeney / JAI (bl). **68 Alamy Images:** Steffen Binke (cra); Worawan Simaroj (bl); Travelscape Images (br). **Corbis:** Jose Fuste Raga (cl). **Dorling Kindersley:** Barnabas Kindersley (tr). **Getty Images:** Eye Ubiquitous / Universal Images Group (clb). **Science Photo Library:** Diccon Alexander (ca). **69 Alamy Images:** Douglas Fisher (ftr); Alida Latham / Danita Delimont (tr); Michael DeFreitas Pacific (cr); Sean Sprague (fbl). **Getty Images:** Auscape / UIG (fcra); Ben Davies / LightRocket (tl); Chris Jackson (fclb). **70 Dorling Kindersley:** Martin Richardson / Rough Guides (br). **77 Alamy Images:** Charles O. Cecil (cl). **Dorling Kindersley:** Paul Whitfield / Rough Guides (cra).

All other images © Dorling Kindersley
For further information see: www.dkimages.com

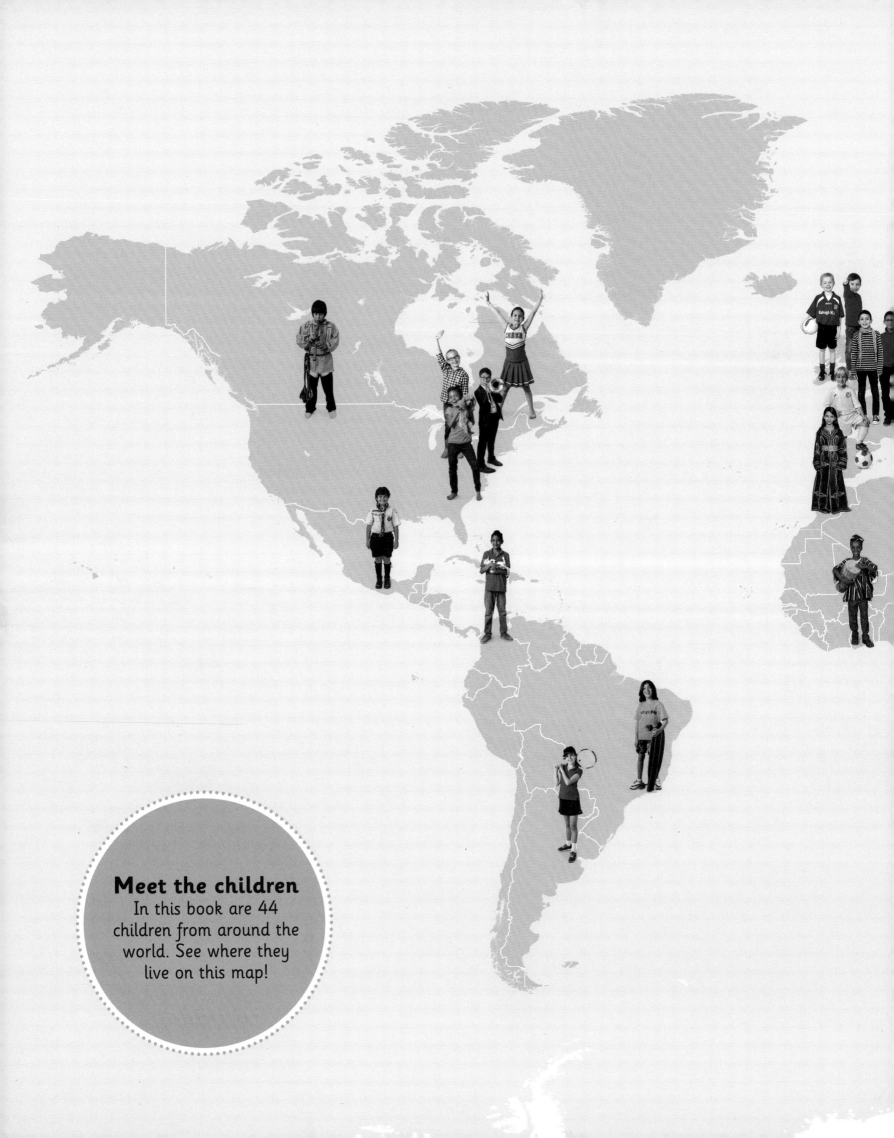

Meet the children
In this book are 44 children from around the world. See where they live on this map!